America's Own Mark Twain

By the Same Author

Published by William Morrow and Company

THE STORY OF ELEANOR ROOSEVELT. 1956

TRUMPETER'S TALE, the Story of Young Louis Armstrong.
1955

LEE, the Gallant General. 1953

WASHINGTON, the Nation's First Hero. 1951

GANDHI, Fighter Without a Sword. 1950

BUCKEY O'NEILL OF ARIZONA. 1949

THAT LIVELY MAN, BEN FRANKLIN. 1948

DAVID LIVINGSTONE, Foe of Darkness. 1947

BETSY'S NAPOLEON. 1936

Published by Harcourt, Brace and Company

LONE JOURNEY. 1944

NARCISSA WHITMAN. 1941

LEADER BY DESTINY. 1938

America's Own
Mark Twain

JEANETTE EATON

Illustrated by LEONARD EVERETT FISHER

WILLIAM MORROW & COMPANY
New York   1958

To

JOHN E. WILFONG

and

HIS HERMITAGE

America's Own Mark Twain

CHAPTER · · · · · · · ONE

One warm afternoon in May, 1840, the village of Hannibal in eastern Missouri seemed sound asleep. There was no one to be seen on the dusty main street except several loafers dozing on benches in front of a shabby tavern, nothing to be heard except the tap, tap of a cobbler's hammer, the faraway squealing of pigs in the slaughterhouse pen and the screech of a jay from nearby woods.

Only sharp ears could have heard the sound of a child's merry laughter, rising from the grass plot beside a two-story frame house. There a five-year-old boy with reddish curls was playing with a tiger kitten. With a lilac branch drawn teasingly first right, then left, he induced the kitten to leap and pounce in a hunter's ecstasy.

11

As the long, sustained bellow of a steam whistle shattered the stillness, the startled kitten scurried to shelter. The boy sprang up and dashed through the gate into the road. The village resembled a disturbed ant hill. Heads poked out of windows and women leaned from doorways. Market Street was already a stream of men, children, and dogs running down the steep hill. That whistle heralded the great event of any day for Hannibal. A steamboat was arriving! Perched on the steep bank of the Mississippi River, the town was a regular stop for boats plying up and down.

In that era the Mississippi was the continent's great artery. Fur traders, pioneers, missionaries, and businessmen were continually traveling north and south. So was cargo. Molasses, rice, sugar, and tobacco came from New Orleans, and merchandise from St. Louis. Small settlements along the way were also active shippers. Lumber, wheat, fowl, hemp, pork, and eggs were the usual products. No wonder the deep-voiced whistle was thrilling. Steamers brought bits of the world to towns like Hannibal.

The little boy's swift zigzag through the hastening crowd was halted by a heavy hand on his shoulder. "Well, Sammy Clemens," a voice boomed, "guess you're in a hurry to get cargo from St. Louis, ain't you!"

Sam looked up at a man the youngsters considered the town's leading citizen, for he kept a candy store. With an appreciative grin, the boy drawled, "Sure, Mr. McDaniel. I'm lookin' for a pony an' a pony cart to come today."

The man's fingers dug into Sam's shoulder. "Saints alive, boy! Anybody'd think you was the pork packer's son with cash to burn. Does your pa know? Bet Judge Clemens'll be more upset than ever."

Sam shot a bewildered glance at the speaker. Why wasn't he laughing at a plain joke? Wrenching himself free, he tore along to watch the majestic vessel sliding against the dock. The pilot was ringing bell signals to the engineer. From the bridge the captain looked down smiling. Passengers had massed on deck to watch the lowering of the gangplank. Stevedores were lined up, ready to unload and load cargo.

Perching himself on the last tall post of the wharf, Sam Clemens watched, listened, and kicked his bare heels in excitement. With a final whirl of paddles the huge boat lay quiet, with ropes wound fast around posts fore and aft. From the noisy, milling crowd, the boy's eyes sought the pilot. He was leaning from his window with an imperious air which asserted that he, not the captain, was master of the ship. Every time Sam looked up during the next fifteen minutes, he found the pilot's expression unchanged. How marvelous, he thought, to be such a king!

As the steamboat backed away and the people on the wharf began to scatter, Sam heard his name shouted by a familiar voice. "Sam! Come on home! Mother wants you." At the edge of the dock a tall, handsome boy looked up with a worried frown. Receiving no attention whatever, he gave one dangling little bare foot a vigorous shake.

The foot kicked and squirmed. "Aw, quit, Orion. Leave me be. What does Ma want?"

"Don't know. Come down. Trot home and find out."

With a look of fury Sam slipped to the dock. At the same moment a man's voice called out, "Where's your pony, Sam? I didn't see him put off."

The little boy's clouded face lit up. "Guess he's coming on the next boat, Mr. McDaniel. He'd better. I'm going to ride him clear out to Uncle John's farm."

As the candy-store owner moved away with a grave shake of the head, Orion turned a glare of disapproval upon his brother. "What on earth is this about a pony?" he asked.

Sam tossed him an impish look and began to scamper up the hill. Orion's long legs kept pace. As the boys approached the frame house on Hill Street, Sam said, between panting breaths, "You're always readin' books, Orion, but you don't learn nothin'—at least, you don't about jokes."

Before Orion could defend his sense of humor, the pair had entered the kitchen. The small room already held three children. Pamela, a girl of thirteen, sat at the kitchen table holding two-year-old Henry on her lap. Beside her, stroking the baby's cheek, was Benjamin, aged seven. At the stove stood a Negro slave girl named Jenny. With a long wooden spoon in hand, she looked around to grin a welcome to the newcomers. But the dominant figure in the room was the children's mother. Slender and charming in her ruffled calico dress, she set down a bowl of frothy egg whites and turned her bright head toward the door.

Reproof struggled with relief and affection as she said slowly, "Sam Clemens, where have you been this last hour? I told you, sonny, not to go out of the yard. You're still weak from the awful stomach-ache you had last night."

Without response Sam stooped to snatch up his playmate, the tiger kitten. It was Orion who answered. "He was down at the wharf, sitting on a post, Ma, and he got mad when I made him come home."

"Well, anyway, he's here," responded his mother cheerfully. "Now it won't be long till supper's ready. Suppose you children pack yourselves into the other room, and, Pamela, honey, will you please set the table?"

Immediately Benjamin, lifting the baby from his sister's lap, guided the toddler through the doorway. Orion and Pamela followed. Sam, however, merely dropped into a dark corner of the kitchen with the kitten in his arms. Nor did he stir when a tall man in a snuff-brown swallow-tailed coat opened the door, took off his high beaver hat, and nodded to his wife.

"Evening, John," she said pleasantly.

"Good evening, Jane." The tone matched the weary motions of hanging his hat on a peg and sinking into a chair.

As Sam watched his father, Mr. McDaniel's remark sprang up in his mind. What did he mean about his father's being so upset? Was anything the matter?

Indeed there was! Ever since John Marshall Clemens

was a boy he had had to struggle to earn enough to pay family debts and make a living. He and his wife had both grown up in Kentucky. When they married he had, as they said, "prospects." He was trained in the law and had been appointed Justice of the Peace, a post which gave him the title of Judge from then on.

This serious, intelligent man was far from practical. Moving to Tennessee, he tried for years to make his living in first one town and then another. At last he accepted an offer from his brother-in-law, John Quarles, to help him with his store in a Missouri town called Florida. Quarles had a big farm near the village and loved to have the Clemens children come there to play. The partnership in the store, however, did not last. Following this disappointment came the sudden death of beautiful nine-year-old Margaret Clemens, and her grieving parents looked upon the town of Florida as a place of blighted hopes. They decided that a river town was likely to offer more opportunity. Hannibal was their final choice.

On arrival the judge found no immediate chance to practice law. He started a little store and used part of the frame house he rented for lodging travelers. Orion, who helped at the store, had even less business sense than his father. Now, after nearly a year in Hannibal, debts had piled up. This was partly due to a loan which the innocent judge had made to a rascal who would not pay it back. Because misfortunes were never discussed, the children were unaware of them. But the grave, silent man who appeared at meals sometimes cast a puzzling shadow over the exuberant household. Often its members almost forgot he was there. It was his talkative, radiant, temperamental wife to whom the family turned.

This evening she told them about a letter from her brother-in-law, John Quarles. "He wants us—as many as can come—to stay at the farm this summer," she reported. Smiling at the chorus of delight from Pamela and Benjamin, she said to her husband, "I think it will be good for Sam, John. He'll work up an appetite there. Look at him! Look at that plate! He's hardly eaten anything, and we're ready for the lemon pie."

Sam came out of his dreamy silence with an excited burst of questions. "When do we go, Ma? Tomorrow? Is it far?"

"Well, it's about forty miles from here. Don't you remember that the farm is near Florida, where you were born? No, we're not going yet, sonny. It takes time to get ready. And now look here, if you don't drink your milk you don't deserve to come along."

Orion had been swaying restlessly in his chair during this conversation. Well he knew that as assistant storekeeper, he would not be taken to the farm for the summer. To change the unbearable topic, he announced that the missionary society meeting at the Bowen family's house that evening was to have a banjo player from the county seat. "Likely there'll be singing," he declared. "Maybe people will even dance."

"Dance!" Mrs. Clemens' eyes sparkled. "Oh, that very word makes my toes wiggle. Guess I'll just have to go. Will you go too, John?"

The judge half smiled, as if remembering how he had once loved to dance. But he shook his head. "No, Jane. Tonight I wish to work a bit on my perpetual-motion machine."

His wife sighed. Her husband was forever tinkering with some crazy invention. Tossing her head, she declared that Orion would escort her in his place. After appointing Pamela guardian of the two small boys, she picked up little Henry, already half-asleep, and hurried upstairs to dress.

Sam observed with mischievous intent how kindly his parents had disposed of themselves. The moment Orion and his mother had set forth, he whispered to Pamela, "Let's you and me and Benjamin go get Jenny to tell us stories."

At their home in Florida Jenny had been well trained in storytelling. She always joined the children when on winter evenings an ancient Negro slave, the household's man of all work, regaled them with legends as old as Africa. It was one of his shivery tales which Jenny related that night to the three children. It involved a haunted house and a wicked witch who made a ball of fire and hurled it at a stranger riding by.

"That man couldn't lose the fire ball no matter how fast he galloped," related Jenny, in a tone filled with fear. After a long description of his terrible ride homeward, she con-

cluded, "At last he reached his own place and his wife was at the door. When she looked out and saw that big ball of fire blazing away, she screamed, 'That's devil fire!' "

Leaning forward in terror at Jenny's screech, Sam asked, "And then what did she do?"

"She quick worked a witch's spell that she knew. She waved her arms an' she speak the words of that spell. An' all at once the ball of fire rolled away—far away—and faded." Jenny's voice trailed off in a whisper.

"Then what?" persisted her youngest listener.

Jenny chuckled. "Then, sure enough, the po' man he put his horse to bed and went to bed himself. An' "—she stood up with her hands extended like claws—"if you don't want that ball of fire rollin' round here, you all git right upstairs and go to bed this minute!"

Later, after his sister had heard him say his prayers, Sam said dreamily, "Guess when we get to Uncle John's farm, old Uncle Daniel will tell us scarier stories than that!" He leaned back against the pillows to conjure up the kindly image of the old Negro with its promise of warm companionship.

Pamela stretched luxuriously. "Oh, everything's such fun at the farm. Now you and Benjamin go to sleep, Sam, and dream about the orchard and all the horses and cows and the good things we'll have to eat."

Sam did go to sleep, but the ball of fire kept whizzing through his dreams and waking him up. He was sure the blazing horror followed him because he had not obeyed his mother by staying in the yard.

When he appeared at breakfast next morning, Mrs. Clemens was shocked at his pallor. She determined to hurry preparations for the summer visit with her sister and John Quarles. In a week the great day of departure dawned. Just before sunrise she tucked the four children into the big wagon with luggage and a huge basket of food. Orion, Judge Clemens, and Jenny waved them good-by.

As the wagon rattled down the street, Sam's mother turned to look at him. "That child has a mighty innocent air," she remarked dryly to Pamela. "It probably means he's planning mischief."

At the Quarles farm innocent mischief was taken for granted. Aunt Patsy and Uncle John were a warm, affectionate, hospitable pair. With their little daughter Tabitha, they welcomed the five guests with hugs and kisses and took them in to a stupendous dinner.

As soon as Sam and Benjamin had finished their dessert, they were allowed to slip off with Tabitha to roam the farm. Across the enormous yard, past hickory and walnut trees, then down a long slope, they skipped to the big barn. There a young Negro, engaged in harnessing a pair of horses to a hay wagon, grinned a greeting. "You all like to go out to the field in the wagon? We're cuttin' hay early this year." He was answered by shouts of joy.

Before he scrambled into the wagon with the others, Sam patted each horse and asked its name. This seemed to please the driver. The wagon rattled its way along the orchard to the clover field. A group of Negroes at work there

rested on their scythes to call out, "Howdy, chilluns!"
And laughed to watch their desperate scramble up the first
huge stack of grass and clover. Even the havoc wrought on
their well-shaped stack seemed to amuse them. When the
wagon was loaded, the children were helped to climb on top
of it for the ride back.

After exploring the barn, Benjamin suggested that they
find whether the swing hanging from a branch of a chest-
nut tree at the edge of the orchard was still there. " 'Course
it is!" cried Tabitha indignantly, and led a race to the
spot. They took turns swinging under the tall tree. When
Sam was given his sail through the air, he kept shouting,
"Higher, higher, Ben! I want to touch the sky!"

Next came a visit to the slave quarters. Pamela, who had
joined the others, demanded that they call first at Aunt
Susanna's cabin.

Sam, dipping into his memory of other visits, asked,
"Is she the one that's so old?"

Eagerly his companions repeated the facts learned from
the Negroes. Pamela said that Aunt Susanna must be
at least a thousand years old, because she had seen Moses
with her own eyes. Benjamin declared she had crossed the
Red Sea when it rolled back to let the Children of Israel
pass safely out of Egypt. Tabitha asserted that she had
magic powers, but had always used them to do good.

Admitted to the cabin by a dark-skinned young woman,
the children tiptoed to the bed, where under spotless
covers lay the shriveled form of the ancient woman. They

gazed with awe at the wrinkled brown face and were startled when she opened a pair of glittering eyes to glance
from one to the other.

With the faint ghost of a smile she put a withered hand
on Sam's curly head. "De sun mus' always shine on you!"
she murmured, and closed her eyes again.

As they slipped outdoors, Sam boasted happily, "She
picked me out, didn't she?"

The double line of log cabins for the colored families
had the aspect of a tiny village. Young women with babies
in their arms came out to greet the children and exclaim,
"Land o' goodness, how you've grown!" Older women
hanging out laundry smiled and waved. Youngsters with
fingers in their mouths stared curiously. Hound dogs
were everywhere. Some were asleep on the trampled grass.
Others, wagging vigorously, came sniffing around the
strangers. Sam scratched their long ears and patted their
flea-bitten backs.

Benjamin and Sam found two boys cleaning a gun.
Both sprang up in glad surprise. "Heard you was comin'!"
they cried. "If you stay till frost you can go out on a coon
hunt."

The clang of a big bell summoned everyone to wash
hands and face before supper. Fried chicken and early peas,
hot biscuits and strawberry jam, made the rounds. Uncle
John, in roaring good humor, teased each one in turn and
Mrs. Clemens parried with sprightly wit. After supper
Sam and Benjamin hurried off to watch the cows come

back from pasture. One of the older Negro women had the duty of herding them into the milking barn.

In his serene way Benjamin walked quietly beside her down the lane. But Sam skipped ahead, climbed over the fence, and ran among the cows. Paying no heed to the vexed voice of the old woman, he snatched up a stick and rushed the startled beasts so fast that she could hardly get the gate open before they dashed through. Laughing wildly, Sam jumped up and down as the cows went snorting past him.

"You're kind of a crazy young-un, ain't you!" said the old woman. Yet her toothless grin showed that she knew a boy's wild high spirits were like those of a wayward calf in spring.

During those wonderful three months at the farm, the children tiptoed out to help feed chickens and gather eggs each morning at sunrise. They learned to ride the sober work horses out to pasture. On hot days the boys sneaked off to the creek, where before long they were transforming mere splashing into attempts at swimming. The sport was forbidden by their mother, and sometimes Sam's damp curls and unusually clean face brought down upon him a sharp scolding and some well-contrived punishment.

Gladly he paid that price. What arose in the depths of his young soul that summer was a passion for freedom of action which dominated every other emotion. Benjamin merely followed his inventive small brother, and for the most part the projects were completely innocent. Exploring the woods, hunting for wild blackberries, playing games with the Negro children, helping themselves to apples and watermelon, climbing trees, racing down the hillsides—these formed the pattern of enchanted hours. Every week Mrs. Clemens noticed Sam's improved health and strength. He ate his meals with enthusiasm, slept without dreaming, and grew strong of muscle. In the Quarles household, with its atmosphere of ease and good humor, there existed no obstacle to happiness.

When the sad day of departure came, Sam was inconsolable. "It's like leaving heaven!" he wailed.

CHAPTER · · · · · · · TWO

It was school that Sam dreaded. The very next day after the family was reunited at Hannibal he had to set out to the little log house on Main Street. Mrs. Elizabeth Horr was the teacher—the keeper of Sam's jail. From afar he saw her standing in the doorway to greet her pupils with a smile. But she and Sam met in a spirit of mutual suspicion. "Here is the mischief-maker" was the message of her glance. His sulky pout declared, "The old tyrant looks as mean as ever."

As he plumped down on a bench at the back of the room he rehearsed his first day of school the year before. During the first hour he had pulled so many pigtails, tickled so many boys' shins, and made so many funny faces to inspire giggles that Mrs. Horr used up her complete store of reproofs and sent him out to get a switch for his own punishment. After a long disappearance he returned with a fragile shaving which had blown into the schoolyard from a nearby carpenter's shop. To the accompaniment of general laughter he gravely handed it to his teacher.

"Samuel Langhorne Clemens," she cried. "I'm ashamed of you." Immediately she had sent one of the bigger boys out to cut something that looked like a switch. It felt like one, too, as it descended on Sam. Since he had never suffered such a punishment at home, he raged inwardly at the indignity. From then on he spent most of his school hours in planning vengeance. He became such an adept at contriving mischief which could not be pinned on him that his punishments were actually few. Facing his second year now, he wondered how the battle would go.

Classes always began with a prayer and a reading from the Bible. These selections, like the sermons Sam heard on Sundays, usually dealt with sinners and their awful fate. The Book of Job was a favorite choice. Sternly Mrs. Horr would read a passage describing God's punishment of a wicked person.

"He shall flee from the iron weapon, and the bow of steel shall strike him through. A fire that no man lit shall consume him. The heavens shall reveal his iniquity; and the earth shall rise up against him."

Listening with inward shudders, Sam felt tumult in his soul. On the one hand, he became convinced that God was only a fierce avenger. On the other, he had a guilty feeling that his own iniquities might justly be written on the sky and that fire might well devour him. However, once the arithmetic lesson began, such dark forebodings vanished, and he gleefully pulled the pigtail of the little girl in front of him.

Almost against his will the little rebel learned to read that year. That helped long winter days to pass swiftly. Bad colds and stomach upsets that kept him home proved boons to learning. Basking in his mother's anxious care, he pored over tales of adventure. Spring days with windows open were the enemies of schoolbooks. Then ears and eyes attended only to the trill of warblers, bursting cherry blossoms, and drifting sunlit clouds. During the recreation periods in the yard, however, he abandoned dreams to chase the girls, fight enemies, and cement friendships with boys who admired his pranks. Sometimes, with one or two other daring truants, he would slip away to visit the river or steal into the woods to spy on old Indian Joe's tumble-down cabin.

It was the May Day celebration, put on belatedly in June, which aroused sudden loyalty to the school. For this occasion boys were dressed in their Sunday jackets and best nankeen pants. Girls wore ruffled dresses just short enough to show embroidered pantalets. To the toot and thump of the municipal band, the pupils marched along Main

Street, which was lined with applauding parents and lesser citizens. A Maypole dance, songs, and declamations by the older children were performed in the grassy corner of an ancient graveyard. The finale was a lavish picnic dinner spread for the heroes and heroines of a nine-month scholastic struggle.

In May, 1842, however, no one in the Clemens family had the heart to join the celebration. Benjamin, the gentlest, sweetest-tempered member of the family, was suddenly stricken with a mortal illness. On the night Sam learned from Pamela that their brother could not get well, he tossed all night in despairing sleeplessness. Before him arose every occasion when he had teased Ben or persuaded him to mischief. The realization that he could never redeem such wickedness was crushing. Early in the morning he tiptoed into the room where his brother lay. One glance at the sheeted figure told him that Benjamin was dead. His mother sat beside the cot with her head in her hands.

In a soundless rush Sam reached her side. "Oh, Ma," he moaned. "Oh, Ma!"

Her soft hand touched his head. In a tear-choked voice she said, "Yes, Sammy, he is gone. We can't understand it. But we can still say, 'The Lord gave and the Lord hath taken away.'" Sam shook his head. He could only kneel in awe and fear and beg forgiveness for all his sins. Weeks passed before he could either sleep or eat normally.

Due to his shattered state, his mother lengthened the summer visit at the Quarles farm to late autumn. The coming of frost brought new sources of delight to Sam. The spacious sitting room was warmed by crackling logs in the huge fireplace and after dark all the family gathered there. Uncle John sat smoking his pipe in a rush-bottomed chair in one chimney corner and Aunt Patsy sat knitting opposite him. Mrs. Clemens worked on a piece of fine embroidery beside the kerosene lamp. Tabitha and Sam and often little Henry and several neighbor children romped and laughed in the shadows.

Three times, when the moon was full, Sam stole off to join the Negroes on a hunt for coons. Excited hounds sniffing, racing, and barking; boys and men with guns and lanterns tramping through the woods; voices calling and the bang of the guns—here were all the elements of a thrilling chase.

On rainy evenings old soft-spoken Uncle Daniel was persuaded to come in and entertain everyone with stories. He could send chills down youthful spines with witch stories. But he himself preferred to relate "How de Mean Old Fox Got His Comeuppance" or "How Bunny Rabbit Done Fooled Mr. Houn' Dog."

When he got home again Sam not only retold to Pamela these fascinating legends, but invented many of his own. When he could make her laugh or bring the glow of interest into her eyes, he would bounce with pride in his creations. He wondered if he could ever inspire an equal response in Orion. This vain hope made him miss Benjamin more than ever. He would have listened!

Orion was no longer in Hannibal. His father had secured him an apprenticeship in a printing firm in St. Louis.
When he came home for holidays he seemed to Sam
strangely old and silent. One evening when his mother
asked him why he was so melancholy, Sam put down his
book to hear the answer.

"Well, Ma," said Orion slowly, "how could you expect
me to like my kind of employment? Our people weren't
laborers like me. How often you've told us how your family
descended from an English earl. And look at Pa! He had
an ancestor who sat in Parliament. Seems to me I ought
to be in a profession."

Tossing her red head, Mrs. Clemens replied, "Yes, our
heritage is of the best—except in one respect. We weren't
left good money to go with good blood, nor even the ability to make it. So we just have to do what we can. I was
brought up to be a fine lady." Instinctively she stretched
out her slender white fingers. "But now I'm going to keep
boarders until things get better for your father. If you
learn the printing trade, Orion, you may reach out to something else. Remember how Benjamin Franklin got on."

A deep voice from the corner of the room said, "Don't
ever forget, my children, our lands in Tennessee. If anything happens to me, you will inherit those one hundred
thousand acres. There are riches in them." Judge Clemens
leaned toward his wife and the lamplight on his face revealed dreamy satisfaction.

With a little shrug, Jane Clemens tossed the vast Tennessee tract into the limbo of illusion. Her husband had

bought it for four hundred dollars not long after they were married and there it lay useless, demanding taxes every year.

Sam stared at his mother's expression of scorn. Why didn't she think it wonderful to own so much land? It was queer that she even hated to have it mentioned. Giving up the puzzle, he spoke to Orion. "Say, I'm going to skate on the river tomorrow with Will Bowen. Want to come along? It's frozen hard clear across to Illinois."

Orion acknowledged the invitation with a gentle smile, but reminded his brother that he had to leave early in the morning with a pork packer who was driving his big wagon down to St. Louis. Everyone turned sorrowing looks upon him. But this was an undemonstrative family and no one said anything. Only his mother was up to give him breakfast at dawn and say good-by. She remained in the kitchen to be sure Sam ate something before he strode off with skates under his arm to speed across the vast ice field of the Mississippi.

With his closest chum, Will Bowen, and several other boys, Sam often spent half the day enjoying this sport. Not only were racing and playing tag exhilarating, there was something wondrous in the sight of the mighty river held motionless in winter's grip. On sunny days the blue sheen of a surface usually a dingy brown, the splendor of clouds overhead, the glitter of frozen branches on the tree-lined shores of mainland and islands, composed a scene of such beauty that even the boys were aware of it.

Uncle John's farm and the great river provided Sam with

a wide variety of enchanting amusements—sometimes mixed with strange and even frightening experiences. In the fall of 1843, for example, Sam was almost scared into believing that truancy was a sin, after a magnificent afternoon of forbidden freedom ended late at night in terror.

A few moments after he had sneaked away from the schoolyard that day, Sam met Tom Blankenship. Tom was the most envied eight-year-old in Hannibal. He didn't go to school. He went barefoot from early spring until snowfall. He could fish, swim, and paddle a canoe all day if he chose. On the other hand, he had no mother and his reprobate of a father often beat him in a drunken rage. He went about unwashed and dressed in rags, he seldom had enough to eat, and sometimes, when his father was drunk, he had to sleep in some overturned barrel. But this untrammeled freedom gave him an aura of romance in the eyes of his contemporaries. Besides, since the mothers of well-brought-up children sternly forbade all association with Tom, it was peculiarly tempting to seek the company of this easygoing, pleasant-tempered, plucky, and highly experienced individual.

"Hi, Tom, where you going?" asked Sam.

"Oh, fishin', I reckon. I got a skiff hid on shore that was washed up in the storm last week. It don't leak much. Wisht you didn't have to go to that old school and could come along."

"Shucks, I'll come! I'm sick of school already after three weeks of it."

It was the perfect afternoon to put conscience to sleep.

Sam liked to be on the Mississippi better than anywhere else in the world. To paddle against the current was exhilarating and to let the boat drift downstream with no effort except steering was blissful. Every time they passed one of the great rafts that carried lumber from the North, shouted greetings were exchanged. Once they had to paddle furiously to avoid the path of a big steamer.

In the shallows each boy caught two fish and in the late afternoon they landed, built a fire, and cooked them. After a delightful swim they stretched out on the grass, chatting or communing in silence. Glorious sunset clouds drifted southward and later a moon rose above the trees. "Say, Tom," asked Sam suddenly, "do you suppose your pa knows where you are?"

"Nope. Anyway he wouldn't care where I was, except maybe he wants me to fetch him a quart of whiskey. What about your folks?"

Ah, there lurked the dregs in this delicious cup. Sam confessed that probably all his family were combing the town to find him. Silently he pictured his arrival at home and the storm of disapproval that would meet him. It was just too much to face. "I know what I'll do," he said. "I won't go home at all. I'll crawl into Pa's law office and sleep there. Maybe in the morning they'll be so glad I ain't drowned or choked to death by Injun Joe that they'll let me off easy."

"That's a good idea," said Tom, and began to shove off the skiff.

At the corner of two shadowy streets they parted with

whispered farewells. Sam found it easy to push up a window in his father's small office. A shabby couch stood right beside it. Kicking off his shoes, Sam stretched out and was asleep in a few seconds. Perhaps it was the bright moonlight slanting through the window that waked him. He sat up with a jerk, looked around, and stared in surprised recognition of his whereabouts.

But what was that on the floor? Choking down a scream, the boy stared at the man's figure stretched out full length on the wooden boards. Who was it? Was he asleep? Couldn't be a robber in this little hole! Just as Sam was able to breathe again, moonlight flooded down on the motionless figure. Oh, heavens! It couldn't be! What he saw was the marble face of a dead man.

Sam got into his shoes and crawled out of the window! Up the moonlit streets he ran a swift race from the dreadful unknown. No light shone in the Clemens house. Steathily he climbed to the upper porch and found his bedroom window wide-open. Soundlessly stripping off his clothes, Sam lay down beside Henry and by a mighty effort kept his tense body from jerking and thrashing about as he lay there, sleepless.

Next morning he screwed up his courage to face his parents. To his surprise, questions and comments were brief. Unasked, they told him of a shocking murder. Two Spanish travelers from the Southwest had hardly landed in Hannibal when they started a drunken brawl. Knives were flashed and one was driven through the breast of the smaller man. Judge Clemens came on the scene in time to

have the murderer caught and dragged into the j̶
judge then consented to give shelter to the dead
his empty office. Today the killer would be charged ̶w̶i̶t̶h̶
the crime.

Sam listened to the account with his stomach rising and
falling. He knew he was going to be haunted by the dead
man's ghost. And so he was, in uneasy dreams. To rid himself of the awful apparition, he tried to be a model pupil
at school and for nearly a month had a perfect record of
attendance.

In the boy's ninth year his father's fortunes improved
somewhat. He built a more convenient small house on Hill
Street and provided Pamela with a piano, on which she
practiced diligently. The family often gathered around to
sing familiar ditties to her accompaniment. Sam, who had
a sweet treble voice, loved these sessions. Watching him,
his mother would remark to her husband that no one
would suspect their angelic-looking son of being the imp
he was.

Sam had gradually drawn around him a group of boys
ready to follow his impetuous lead anywhere at any time.
One of the many exciting opportunities afforded by Hannibal was its famous cave. When the family first moved
into the town Sam heard of its wonders, and while he was
a little tot he had his first glimpse of its dark interior.
Taken by his mother to a church picnic, he was allowed to
join the young people on a visit to the cave. A good-
humored youth promised to look after him.

A walk straight up a hill brought them to the entrance

on its steep side. An unbolted heavy door of oak had been opened for visitors, and they pushed into the large, dusky entrance chamber. Sam's wondering eyes turned from the uneven rocky floor to the dripping walls and up to the rough ceiling.

"Oh, it's a big cave, ain't it!" he exclaimed.

A girl clinging to the young man's arm giggled at this. "Big! Why it's miles long and miles deep, boy! Nobody's ever been all through it. Wait till we light our candles and you'll see."

Down the sloping passage the chattering procession, with candles lifted high to shine on the strange, glistening walls, moved slowly. Sam was shown how one narrow corridor after another opened off the main path. They turned right into a huge cell hollowed out of solid rock and had to retrace their steps. Laughter and talk echoed merrily through the darkness. But as they kept going down, down, down until he felt they must have reached the very center of the earth, the little boy had asked timorously, "Couldn't you get lost in this cave?"

He was told that you could indeed. For this reason visitors always kept close together and carried plenty of candles. Some few persons had managed to find lakes and foaming streams, and precipices that dropped down to indefinite depths. One misstep on the moist, slippery path might mean death. Although Sam said nothing, this information produced a trembling inside of him that did not cease until he was finally led out of the fearsome labyrinth

and could take a deep breath of fresh air and look gratefully around at the sunny meadows. Nevertheless, on the
way home he remarked to his mother that he meant to explore the cave from top to bottom some day.

At the time Mrs. Clemens only laughed at her small son,
but some four years later she remembered the boast with
a sinking heart. One morning her friend Mrs. Bowen came
in with frightening news. Her son Will had inadvertently
revealed that several times after school he had been exploring the cave with Jimmy McDaniel, John Garth, and Sam
Clemens. "Imagine those young fools!" gasped Will's
mother. "They'll get lost some day sure as you live—if not
drowned or smashed up in a fall. What are we going
to do?"

Jane Clemens heard this report with mingled fear and
indignation. For half an hour the two women exchanged
their worries, which was lucky for Sam. By the time he got
back from school his mother had expended most of her
emotion, and she greeted her son in a mood of loving concern.

"Oh, Sam," she concluded, with a sob in her voice, "do
you want to break my heart? Last year you nearly drowned
trying to swim in the river during a storm. Now you want
to get lost forever in the cave!"

Shocked as he was that his cave explorations were no
longer a secret, the boy was touched by his mother's anxiety. "Oh, Ma," he said, "don't take on so. We won't get
lost. We do just the way Theseus did when he went

through the labyrinth after the Minotaur. You remember—
his lady, Ariadne, gave him a silk string and kept one end
herself at the door. All Theseus had to do after killing the
Minotaur was to go back the way the string led. We tie a
strong kite string to a piece of rock on the main corridor
and unwind it while we explore, and then we follow it back
again. We always keep close together. So don't you worry!"

Mrs. Clemens was not impressed. Sternly she forbade
him ever to enter the cave again. Theseus of Hannibal was
appalled. Grownups! What did they know about the thrill
of discovery? Why, only yesterday he and the other boys
had found the prettiest bubbling spring hundreds of feet
below the surface. He would never promise not to explore
the cave. No! Not if he were tortured like the early Chris-
tians. Of course he couldn't announce his defiance. What
he must do was to distract her attention. By extraordinary
good fortune he had the perfect means of doing so.

With his most disarming smile he said, "I'm sorry you
got so scared about me, Ma. I think a lot of you, Ma. I've
got a present for you in my pocket. Hold out your hand!"

Smiling girlishly in pleased expectation, she did so.
Sam's hand came from his pocket and opened within hers.
A scream followed. "What is it? Oh, my heavens, it's a
bat! Oh, you dreadful boy! Oh, the horrid thing!"

As she rushed to the window to fling away her present,
the donor skipped swiftly from the room.

The explorers agreed that it would be diplomatic to
avoid the cave for several weeks. But thanks to their in-

genious leader, they were soon engaged in a most i
ing project. It concerned a monster boulder perc
the very crest of Holliday Hill. Sam's proposal was to dig
it from its deep bed, push it over the brink, and watch it
bounce its long way down. The idea met with warm approval. Armed with borrowed shovels and spades, the boys
met on the hill several times a week. Hours were spent in
work so arduous that if it had been required by parents,
the boys would have revolted in fury.

"This big thing is like an iceberg," muttered Sam one
day, as he peered down the excavation. "Three quarters of
it is underground, same as an iceberg is more'n three quarters below water."

At last one afternoon the cone-shaped monster moved
a little. With cheers the boys smoothed away the front of
the crater they had dug. Slowly the rock fell forward upon
the runway. "Now push!" shouted the boss. So near the
edge of the short, steep precipice, so ready to tumble was
the boulder, that a push by eight sturdy hands was enough
to topple it over the brink. Tense with excitement, the
boys knelt on the cliff's edge to watch the monster's
progress. There were no big trees in its path. Weeds,
bushes, tender saplings went down before it like tooth-
picks. Smaller rocks crumbled under its weight. "Look at
her go!" yelled Sam.

But above the crash of the wild descent rose a frightened
scream from Will Bowen. "Look! A dray is comin' along
the road down there!"

Fear struck chill to four hearts. They were almost afraid to watch. Then they roared with glee. The boulder's momentum, as it reached the last sheer drop, had carried it sailing over the cart like a mammoth bird. It demolished a neat woodpile at the far edge of the lane—and then bounded straight into the side of a small shop! Half the structure collapsed like kindling, and out of the door rushed three terrified workmen.

"It's the cooper's shop!" gasped John Garth.

The horrified boys saw the men turn from their inspection of the ruin to gaze upward at Holliday Hill. With common accord they wriggled into the bushes like crabs.

At last they could safely stand up behind a big oak tree.

"Anyway," panted Sam, "nobody was even hurt!" Challenged as to why he was so sure, he explained. "Why, those men just stood there scratching their heads and looking. If anybody'd been hurt, they'd have carried him out. Just the same, let's get away quick! Grab your shovels and picks!"

Down the far side of the hill the boys scurried. Each agreed to return his borrowed tools and then slip home. Then immediately after supper they would go, one at a time, to see what was left of the cooper's shop. By that time the weird accident of the boulder's fall had become the talk of the town. There were crowds at the scene of destruction. As hour after hour the workmen had related the tale of the sudden crash and their miraculous escape from death, they reaped so many congratulations, so much sympathy, and such lavish promises of aid in restoring the shop that they obviously felt like heroes. Late that evening the boys met in the Bowens' back yard to express in cautious whispers their mutual relief and their triumph in putting through an exciting project.

Nevertheless, a violent thunderstorm that night shook Sam's complacence. Lightning seemed to hover right over his bed. From moment to moment the frightened sinner expected to be struck down. To the howling wind he confessed his guilt and promised that if only his life were spared, he would take no more risks with the life and property of others. The pact did not, however, include re-

nouncing personal risks of his own. Before a year had gone
by he deliberately put his life in grave danger.

In the summer of 1845 measles was the stylish disease in
Hannibal. One by one all Sam's pals were stricken, until
finally he had nobody to play with. Jane Clemens was determined to keep the infection from her household, and
she watched her irrepressible son's every move with the
stern air of an army sergeant. Like other healthy boys with
anxious mothers, Sam was forbidden to leave home. For a
time he accepted boredom and devoted himself to books.
But when he heard that Will Bowen, in spite of equal iso-
lation, had the measles, he resolved to get the disease too.

One day while his mother was busy with dinner, he
went to his friend's house and knocked at the closed door.
Mrs. Bowen refused to let him in. Next he hid in the
Bowens' yard until he saw her go out of the front door,
and then he sneaked up to Will's room. After only ten
minutes of a delightful chat Mrs. Bowen found him and
sternly sent him home. Finally Sam achieved a night assault. He climbed up a wisteria trellis to Will's window,
slipped into the room, undressed, and got into bed beside
him. Their whispered conversation went unheard. Unfortunately he slept late. In the morning he was personally
conducted back to his alarmed mother. Next day he was
covered from head to toe with red spots.

For a while he felt only satisfaction to be sharing the
scourge with his pals. Then as he burned with fever and
his bones ached, he wondered whether he had made a mis-

take. Yet it was interesting to be the center of constant attention. After a week of high fever he learned from his mother's frightened face that she expected him to die, and in a vague way he believed he might. Pamela wore an air of mourning when she came in to feed him soup. Even his father spent some time sitting silently by his bed.

But Sam eventually began to get well. The best part of his convalescence was a long stay at the Quarles farm. He didn't even mind making up for lost lessons at the country school a few miles from the farm. A morning walk through the woods and meadows was charming. The luncheon he carried in his knapsack was always delicious. Moreover, he had a teacher who made history lessons vividly interesting by paying small attention to the dull textbook, which offered only bare facts and hundreds of dates.

CHAPTER · · · · · · · THREE

One Saturday of the next June Sam Clemens made a sudden announcement. "Say, you all. We've just got to have a boat of our own!"

John Briggs, Will Bowen, and Tom Blankenship, who had also been lolling on the bank of Bear Creek after a long swim, sat up to stare at the speaker, their eyes sparkling at his suggestion.

After a dazed moment, Will said, "That sure would be great. We wouldn't have to waste time borrowing a canoe to go over to Glassocks Island. But how on earth—?"

Tom Blankenship, the oldest of the four, answered. "I know a boat we could git—you know, borrow—for three or four months. The man that owns it hardly uses it any. The trouble is, though, it's painted an awful bright red. He could spot it anywheres on the river."

John Briggs snapped his fingers. "Pooh, why couldn't we paint it gray? He'd never know it was his boat."

Shouts of agreement met this inspired solution. Action was taken at once. While two boys set off to "borrow" the boat, two others went after paint and brushes. They met at a snug hiding place on the creek, where willow boughs drooped low. Before the sun went down, an almost invisible gray boat was drying on the bank. After Sunday school next day they gathered again to daub on a second coat. "Looks gray all right," was the general comment. Sam cleaned the paint brushes with care and volunteered to return them, with what was left in the paint can, to the owner. "He might need it tomorrow when he goes to work," he said kindly.

On Monday afternoon the gray boat was launched and a new era of adventures on the river began. For weeks the boys were content to row across to the Illinois shore and land near an orchard of early apples or go over to Glassocks Island for a picnic. Then suddenly Tom Blankenship reduced such exploits to the level of child's play. He arrived at the Bear Creek hiding place one afternoon carrying a big roll of stained and battered canvas. "Hi!" he shouted, in unwonted excitement. "Look what I found under the house. I'm goin' to fix up a sail for us."

Sam leaped into the air. "Now we can be pirates on the high seas!"

Once the ragged canvas was shaped and nailed to a mast made of a long rake handle and firmly set up, the vessel was ready for its career of plunder. Captain Clemens usually stood in the bow to give orders. If he spied a huge raft or a string of scows floating down on the current, he would shout, "Sail ho! After it, my good men! We'll board the merchant ship and bring back treasure!"

The pirates seldom caught up with any sort of craft, and when they did all they got was a waved salutation from the steersman, but they always returned to Bear Creek with enriched imaginations.

"Wouldn't it be great to be real pirates?" sighed Sam one day.

Will Bowen shook his head. "I'd ruther be a pilot any day—a pilot on one of them big steamboats!" A chorus of "So would I" echoed this sentiment. Tom only shrugged. He knew that a boy with so little schooling would never be accepted as a pilot. Sam waited only a moment to accept the verdict. "Yep. That's the best. A pilot is king of the river."

As Sam grew older his mother became resigned to his escapades. She realized that he was now strong of muscle and a powerful swimmer. Of course she often caught him in acts necessitating a thump with her thimble, a box on the ear, or long and eloquent reproval. More often she was amused by his antics, jokes, and tall tales. Moreover, she trusted the goodness of his heart.

One day at the Quarles farm Sam came rushing into

her room in a fury against a Negro boy who had been hired
by John Quarles from the man who owned him. "Ma," he
roared, "that fella sings and whistles and shouts all day
long. You've got to tell him to quit."

Mrs. Clemens put down her sewing and looked gravely
at her son. "Let me tell you about that little slave boy,
Sammy. His father and mother were sold this summer to
planters way down near New Orleans. He's all alone, nobody to care about him. You ought to be glad he's got the
spirit to sing."

Sam's face grew serious and he murmured with bent
head, "Guess so, Ma. Yep, it's pretty bad for him." After
that he complained no more.

He was never one, however, to express his feelings. His
parents had no way of realizing how deeply any violent
event affected him. Stamped on his soul forever was a
scene he witnessed one day on the square. It began without warning when one of the town characters swayed out
of the tavern. He was a much-liked old fellow, always good-
natured except when he was drunk. Then he would orate
against the misdeeds of men whom he considered enemies,
and his abuse greatly entertained the villagers. Sam and
Jimmy McDaniel, the candy-store owner's son, found him
especially funny.

On this afternoon, however, their merriment died
swiftly. Stamping across the square came a farmer who, as
everyone knew, was the chief target of the old man's abuse.
Day after day, for months, he had been accused of lying,

stealing, and swindling. Now, as the bleary eyes of the drunkard caught sight of him, the usual torrent of vituperation poured forth. This time it reached a man prepared for vengeance. With a single pistol shot, accusation was hushed forever.

Sam couldn't believe what he was seeing. Flat in the road fell the victim, with blood gushing from his chest. An instant afterward the square seethed with men rushing out of stores and houses. Cries and shouts rent the air. The murderous farmer was surrounded. One man had snatched up a Bible as he ran from his house and, stooping over the figure in the road, he laid it on the wounded chest as it heaved its last few gasps.

Glued to the spot by paralyzing panic, Sam had watched the shooting in a fury of protest. Then he saw his father push his way through the crowd. In a voice of quiet command he took charge. The farmer was marched off to jail. Four villagers carried the dead man from the road. Sam could not see where they took him. Feeling dizzy and sick, the boy sank down on the steps of the meat store. In spite of his giddiness, he listened to the conflicting comments of the crowd.

"Serves the old man right!" bellowed one voice. "Jake had taken just about enough insults." Another voice rose in angry protest. "Shooting an unarmed man without no warning is a crime!" But that voice was shouted down by defenders of the farmer's vengeance. As Sam at last dragged himself home, he wondered what his father thought about the tragedy.

To his surprise the judge held forth at length at the supper table. "Rough Western justice, that was!" he said contemptuously. "A lawless criminal act. Yet many of our citizens applauded it. No deed of revenge is justified, let alone anything so awful as murder. But hardly anybody believes that. Mark my words, when this case is tried before a jury, the murderer will go free."

When news came some weeks later from Palmyra, the county seat, it bore out this prophecy. The farmer was acquitted. Sam's reflections on the matter were not flattering to the human race. He was outraged by the whole episode.

Luckily such grim happenings were few. Hannibal was not really a pioneer town and was usually a peaceful one. The citizens were easily thrilled by a church picnic, the yearly visit of a little circus, or the unexpected arrival of a show boat with minstrels and a calliope shrilling out *The Last Rose of Summer* and *Gaily the Troubadour*. The Fourth-of-July parade and celebration with orations were the pride of the town and so was the New Year's Day open house held by the mayor, to which even the children were invited. Sam's gang joyfully attended all these entertainments. But unlike their hard-working elders, they made every day an enthralling adventure. A region that offered a deep swimming hole in the creek, a fascinating river highway, and a weird cave with a legendary treasure of hidden gold was a paradise for exuberant youth.

It never occurred to Sam that this happy existence wouldn't last forever. He was twelve years old before he had to face a profound change in his way of life. It was not caused by poverty, for all the Clemens family were used to that. Sam didn't even mind when they had to give up their house and move into cramped quarters over a store, because there was an upstairs window that opened on a porch, and it was convenient for slipping out to join his companions for a midnight enterprise.

It was sorrow that rocked the foundations of Sam's boyhood happiness. Yet the year of 1847 had started well. Judge Clemens was slated for the position of clerk of the Circuit Court, with a fixed salary. At the family dinner table he discussed a plan for a better house. Even the sale of part of the Tennessee lands seemed possible in such an atmosphere of optimism.

The change came suddenly. In March, on a trip back from Palmyra, the judge was chilled to the bone by a sleet storm. At once his lungs became congested and a fever mounted dangerously. Pamela, Henry, and even Sam did what they could to help their mother. Finally she sent for Orion to come home and assist her with the nursing. Dark shadows closed over the household.

Tossing sleepless on the night when his father died, Sam asked in despair why such sorrows came upon his family— first Margaret, then Benjamin, and now his father. When he stood with his mother beside the coffin, vivid memories swept before him of his father's dignity, kindness, and brave efforts to surmount trials and failures.

As if she were aware of these thoughts, his mother said, "He was a good man, Sam, none more upright, none more

hard-working. Promise me, son, that you'll be good and true like your father."

Sam clenched his hands against the bitter pain of knowing that he had not loved or obeyed his father as he should have done. "Oh, Ma, yes. I promise. I'll work for you. I'll do anything. Only—please, Ma, don't make me go to school any more."

With a faint smile Mrs. Clemens shook her head. Well she knew that a boy who could race through books and stand at the head of his class in spelling could profit by more study. Sam continued to attend the school for older boys—a vast improvement, in his opinion, over Mrs. Horr's

classes. Then, after a glorious vacation at the Quarles
farm, which was even more fun this time, because Henry
was old enough now to join in sports and pranks, Sam
undertook jobs every afternoon and on Saturdays. They
consisted of errands for storekeepers and delivery of the
Gazette to subscribers.

Although he was proud of handing his puny earnings to
his mother, it was hard to have his hours of play so cir-
cumscribed. Members of the gang were inconsolable. "It's
no fun without you!" they complained to him. Tom
Blankenship would have been more sympathetic if he had
not felt such contempt for Sam's growing interest in girls.

"What I can't figger out," he said, "is when you only
got evenin's and Saturday afternoons and Sundays to go
fishin' and skatin' and diggin' in the cave, you waste time
on gals."

Actually Sam had always spent time and attention upon
the fair sex. His first romantic emotions had been inspired
by young ladies the age of his sister Pamela. Later his
sweethearts were usually the slightly younger sisters of his
best friends. From them he learned about the feminine
readiness for jealousy. Just let him turn away, no matter
how briefly, from the girl of the moment, and she would
first pout and then openly jilt him for some other boy. Nor
would she be reconciled until he had fervently begged her
forgiveness.

The drama of the situation fascinated him. Swiftly he
learned to copy the technique. He would pretend to Jennie

that he was going to take Mary to the Fourth-of-July picnic, or break the news to Mary that he had decided to take another girl to the moonlight party on the ferryboat. Sometimes the girls combined to attack him. "Sam Clemens, you're the meanest boy in the whole world!" they would cry.

Nothing could have been more innocent than such games of advance and retreat. Hannibal was ruled by the Southern tradition that women were to be worshiped and protected. The wildest boys wouldn't have dreamed of swearing in the presence of girls. To take any liberties would have been unthinkable. The swift exchange of a kiss in the moonlight was the culmination of the romantic mood. Sam enjoyed making his current sweetheart blush over his extravagant compliments, but was better pleased when she laughed at his jokes.

This ingrained respect for women heightened the whole town's horror over a sensational episode that year. Sam and Tom Blankenship, returning by way of Holliday Hill from a raid on an apple orchard, were the first witnesses of the shocking scene. As they drew near the isolated house of a much respected widow, known to all for her good works, they heard the sound of rough voices. In amazement they stopped to listen. One voice came clear. A man was shouting that the widow must let them in, or he and his partner would break down the door.

Sam clutched Tom's arm. "Who on earth are they?" he whispered.

"Must be them two devils what landed in town yesterday. They've been roarin' drunk most of the time. They're plenty dangerous."

Stepping carefully, the boys halted under a big oak tree near the house. The yells and threats had become more savage. One of the pair, a huge, tall man, was poised for a rush up the porch steps. At that instant the door of the house was flung open. Silhouetted against the lamplight stood the widow. In her hands was a hunting gun, aimed at the intruder.

"You all leave here this minute or I'll shoot!" The widow's voice was resolute. Her gun was ready.

At once the smaller man began staggering down the hill. But the other put a booted foot on the porch step, crying, "Put down that gun and let me in!"

"I'm counting three!" answered the intrepid woman. "Git out or I'll fire!"

A roar of derisive laughter met the threat. Frozen in suspense, the two boys listened to the deliberate count. "One—two—three!" There was a blast of gunfire, and the man crumpled, fell, and rolled a few feet down the slope.

Instantly Sam and Tom leaped to the porch. The woman lowered the smoking gun and set it down against the door. Stepping inside, she sank into a chair, fixed staring eyes on the boys, and muttered, "I killed a man. Oh, Lord, forgive me! I had to, I had to. I got nobody to protect me."

Now voices could be heard, and the tramp of feet hastening up the hill. Lanterns flashed through the dark. There was a shout as the villagers found the dead man on the path. In another moment the widow's house was crowded. Over her limp form bent anxious faces. Like hornets the questions buzzed around her.

"Ask them two boys," she said, in a choked voice. "I'm fair done in!"

This was the beginning of unusual notoriety for Sam and Tom. Tonight for the villagers, tomorrow at the mayor's office, and later in court, they testified that the widow had fired in imperative self-defense. Of course they found themselves the envy of all the boys in town, and Sam made the most of the opportunity to swagger.

For a year after her husband's death, Mrs. Clemens had struggled to support her family. She kept a boardinghouse and did all the cooking. But even though Pamela gave piano lessons to reluctant little girls and Orion sent a weekly sum from St. Louis, there was not enough money to clothe the children and herself and pay interest on debts. Sam's contribution of nickels and pennies earned after school did little to swell the family's funds. A new source of income had to be found. At the end of May Mrs. Clemens had a talk with Sam. She tried to soften her decision by telling him that at last he could have his wish to quit school, but he knew instantly that she meant he must go to work. She reported that a man from Palmyra had bought the *Gazette* and was about to start a new weekly in

Hannibal, called the *Missouri Courier*. She told Sam that he must apply for an apprenticeship at once.

When he returned from his first interview with Joseph Ament, the publisher, the look on his face wrung his mother's heart. Steeling herself, she asked in her bright voice what the terms of the printing apprenticeship were.

"Oh, Ma," he replied forlornly, "I gotta live with the Aments for a whole year—eat and sleep there except, maybe, on Sunday. Two older boys do the same thing. And I don't get any pay at all, only meals and two suits of clothes. Ma, I don't like Mr. Ament. He's mean."

Shocked as she was, Mrs. Clemens firmly faced the situation, for it meant that she would have one less person to feed and clothe. She reminded her son that he would be learning something "mighty useful," and she expressed the hope that he might have more time off than he believed. Yet when Sam started from home with his little bag of belongings, she went into the kitchen and wept.

It was the companionship of the other two apprentices which helped Sam to bear the hardships of his first job. They all had to sleep on pallets unrolled on the floor of the printing shop, and eat in the kitchen with the cook and her daughter. Food was scanty and greasy. Sam never looked at his plate without a tantalizing memory of the meals served at the Quarles farm. Work began with sweeping the shop and building a fire. Slowly the boys learned to sort type, make paste, carefully oil the metal plates, and wash the rollers. They folded the printed copies of the *Courier* and delivered them to subscribers.

At first the only relief Sam had from homesickness and rebellion was the older boys' lighthearted acceptance of everything. Wales McCormick, a young giant, was the most fun-loving creature Sam had ever met. Although Pat McMurry lacked invention, he delighted in the pranks of the others. After a few months Sam astounded his companions by his increasing interest in the technique of printing. Indeed, he became such a perfectionist that he often worked until midnight to correct poor punctuation, spelling, and paragraphing.

"You're a pair of blasted dolts," he would growl. "You'd misspell *cat* if you could. I never saw such sloppy work." Then he would have to laugh as Wales, towering over him, threatened to drown him in the inkpot.

Always eager to get back at the little redhead, the older boys gleefully ferreted out his secret. Sam liked to print on a silk ribbon a poem sticky with sentiment to be sent to one of his sweethearts. Wales stealthily captured one such poem and read it aloud. McMurry roared with laughter while the poet jumped up and down like a puppy, trying to reach big McCormick's thieving hand.

Unfortunately for all concerned, the *Missouri Courier* hardly ever printed national news. For example, there was only casual and ironic mention of the amazing migration of the Mormons. Persecuted and chased from state to state, courageously braving the unknown West, this religious group managed to found in Utah, near Great Salt Lake, a settlement destined to become the finest city of the period west of the Mississippi.

As for the growing opposition to slavery in the North, the *Courier's* entire staff and all its readers belittled it with scorn and anger, like most Missourians. To them, an abolitionist was a servant of the devil. Even preachers said so. When Sam discovered that his unpredictable brother Orion had become an ardent believer in the abolition of slavery, he was appalled. Just suppose this became known in Hannibal! The Clemens family would be disgraced.

Naturally Sam had heard about the Mexican War. In the spring and fall of 1847 he had caught from his elders the thrill of pride in the nation's victory. Hannibal now had its first telegraph wire, and at least the most important news filtered through. After the Mexican surrender citizens learned of the acquisition of California. But that meant little until they heard about the discovery of gold near Sacramento. Then, indeed, the town sizzled with interest. Gold was a particularly popular topic, because nobody wished to mention the epidemics spreading in the region. Cholera and yellow fever were taking a fearful toll of the population. Sam couldn't bear to meet the steamers at the wharf during those dark days, because they always unloaded for burial the bodies of passengers who had died on board. Now the shimmering word *gold* turned men's minds from sorrow to dreams of wealth.

One afternoon Sam rushed into the pressroom, shouting, "Come out quick, fellows! Three teams have come, with men goin' to California to dig for gold!"

Dozens of villagers had gathered around the wagons

with eager questions. The men had driven from a northern section of Missouri to take a steamer down to St. Louis, where a steamboat would carry them up the Missouri River to the North Platte. Then by wagon they would follow the old Santa Fé trail to their goal at Sacramento. Beaming under their broad-brimmed felt hats, the emigrants boasted of riches to come. Sam climbed over the wheel of a wagon to gaze at the pickaxes and shovels, the boxes of food and bundles of hay. "Come and git in, Redhead!" laughed the driver. "Make your fortune along with us."

That was the beginning of what a journal called California yellow fever. Every few weeks caravans came through Hannibal. Some of the fortune hunters were not taking the fearful trek across the continent; they chose instead the long water route around Cape Horn and up to San Francisco. Already, it was said, San Francisco was booming, because the forty-niners were trooping there to try their luck and those who succeeded spent gold nuggets as if they were pennies.

Sam and his friends were electrified by the news that John Robard, son of the flour miller, was going with his father to the California gold fields. The boys gathered at the wharf to bid him farewell. Some fifteen other people made up the party. Choked with envy, the boys encircled John to stare at his high boots and plaid shirt and big felt hat. With a swaggering air the future miner boasted of his coming wealth.

"Shucks!" exclaimed Sam. "Bet we'll find more gold in the cave than you'll bring back. Bet you'll be captured by Indians!"

John only laughed good-humoredly. After he had climbed aboard the steamer he came out on deck to wave good-by. All the boys shouted, "Good luck!" And back came the triumphant reply, "I'm off to see the world!" This confident forecast of adventure rang in Sam's ears all the way back to the dreary printing shop. Then his eye caught sight of the page on which he had been writing one of the humorous pieces he was allowed to publish, and with a grin of satisfaction, he sat down to finish it.

In spite of his limited opportunities for reporting and composing, Sam found his apprenticeship increasingly bearable. Moreover, by contrast, it made his hours on the river and exploring the cave more absorbing than ever. A new kind of excitement had also seized upon him. As he walked down the village road one evening, to have supper with the family, he received a strange gift from the wind. A printed page torn from a book was whisked to his feet by a sudden breeze. He picked it up curiously and began reading it as he walked along. Was this a page from a story? Or could it be telling about an actual person? Snatching open the door of the kitchen, he hardly waited to greet his mother before rushing to find Henry and ask, "Was there ever a real girl named Joan of Arc?"

Henry, like Orion, was an impassioned reader. He gave his ignorant brother such a glowing account of the famous

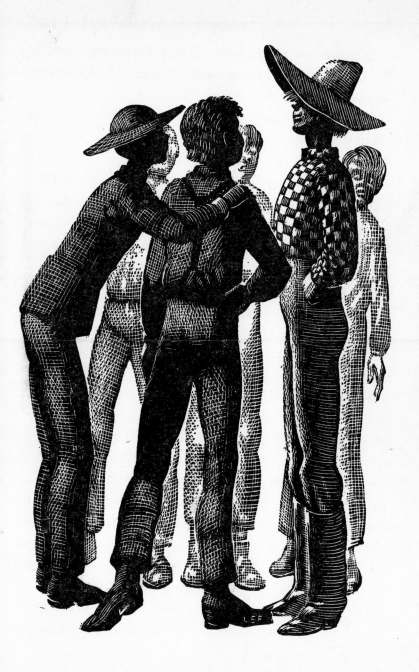

Maid that Sam borrowed a biography of her from the village library. It thrilled him more than any other book he had read. He dreamed of Joan and pondered her fate. To discover if all the biographer said was true, he began reading histories of England and France during the fifteenth century. Although history books were dull and pompous when Sam was a boy, he was too absorbed to be critical. He spent hours with Henry discussing the merits of a king or the wretchedness of the peasants.

Both his devotion to reading and his increasing skill at typesetting helped to prepare Sam for a new family project, engineered by Mrs. Clemens. Having learned that there was a chance to acquire the *Courier's* competitor, the *Hannibal Journal*, she persuaded Orion to buy it with his savings and come back to Hannibal to run it. As soon as he finished his term of apprenticeship, Sam joined his brother. His wages were to be three dollars and fifty cents a week, and to a boy who had earned nothing at all this seemed lordly pay.

However, Orion never gave him a cent. This was partly because of Orion's lack of business ability and partly because subscribers seldom made money payments. Bills were settled by deliveries of cordwood and cabbages, turnips and apples. Sam was so content at home that he seldom complained, especially since Henry was working with him after school hours. The two boys, forever playing tricks upon each other, had many happy hours together.

An apprentice named Jim Wolfe joined the staff. He

lived with the Clemens family and everyone liked him tremendously. Since he was the shyest creature Sam had ever known, Sam could not resist teasing him. One wintry night when Pamela, now twenty-one, was giving a party attended by her best girl friends, Sam had a unique opportunity to torment the helpless Jim. The two boys shared a room above the kitchen porch, and Sam dared him to climb out on the roof and chase away a pair of cats that were howling at each other. "Those cats are spoiling the party, Jim," he said. "You've got to shoo them away." Jim was too proud to refuse the dare.

Hanging out of the window, Sam watched his friend crawl cautiously over the icy roof. Below, he saw the girls running in and out of the kitchen to watch the cooling of the candy they had made. Slowly Jim edged himself near enough to scare the cats. But suddenly he came to a sheet of ice, and as he tried to creep across it he slipped and went plunging down into the midst of the girls and their pans of candy. Screams of fright from the girls split the night. There was a wild scramble to the safety of the kitchen. Sam rocked with laughter as he watched and listened from the bedroom window. The stunt had turned out better than he could possibly have dreamed.

By the time Jim managed to get back into the room, covered with shame, Sam had reduced his laughter to a mere smile. "Jim," he asked admiringly, "how did you ever think up that way of chasing cats?"

Across Sam's sunny days, only slightly shadowed by his

family's poverty, came one cloud of unadulterated horror. Because he had been involved in the tragedy, he could never bear to have it mentioned.

A wretched tramp, who had tried to steal a ride, was put off the steamboat at Hannibal one afternoon. He was drunk at the time and since he still had some money he could spend at the tavern, he soon became a noisy, troublesome nuisance. The mayor had him locked up in the jail for the night. So seldom did the small log building hold a prisoner that in the early evening Sam and Tom Blankenship went down to take a look at him.

Between the iron bars protecting a small window gazed a bearded red face. "Hey, boys!" called a hoarse voice. "For goodness' sake, gimme a match! I got tobacco and a pipe, but nary a light. Don't leave me in this stinking hole without no smoke for comfort."

Sam pictured the ghastly night ahead for the poor wretch. "Here!" he said, reaching through the bars. "Here's some matches for you."

Three hours later, the sound of an extraordinary commotion startled the neighborhood. Market Street was seething with people on the run, and cries of "Fire!" rose from every throat. The jail was on fire.

Pushing through the crowd, Sam, who had been down at the wharf watching the river traffic with Tom, found two long lines of men passing buckets to and from the town well. A fearful scene confronted the boy's horrified eyes. The wooden jail was a crackling furnace. Water spilling from buckets turned instantly to steam. At the window, etched in leaping flames, was the bearded face of the tramp and faintly above the confusion came his frantic cries for help. In a flash Sam realized that no one could get near enough to the ironbound door to unlock it. Just as he reached the end of the bucket line he saw the face disappear from the window.

There were horrified exclamations from the crowd. "He musta gone to sleep with a lighted pipe!" "One match to the straw mattress coulda started the fire!" "Poor fella, he was too drunk to wake up in time." "Lord save his soul! He's nothin' but a cinder now."

When his wavering legs had brought him home, Sam saw his mother at the gate. Stealthily moving in the shadows, he reached the trellis to the porch, climbed it, and slid into his room. At every step his heart beat out the refrain: "Those matches! I did it. I got him burned up!" All through the tortured hours he heard the tramp's agonized cries. Flames danced around his bed. Fear and guilt. Guilt and fear. He ought to go to the sheriff and confess himself as the murderer. It did not help him to know that his gift had been offered as an act of mercy. It had killed a poor old fellow who had done nobody any harm.

Sam was a haunted boy. For days he could hardly eat. Nightmares wrecked his sleep. He set type and corrected copy in a melancholy trance which mystified Orion and Henry. Pamela and his mother pestered him with anxious questions about his health. Yet no one could wrench an explanation from him. He buried his suffering deep within himself and there it worked upon him without his understanding its effect.

Little by little, of course, life and its joys restored this vigorous boy. Once again he eagerly obeyed the call of the river, the swimming hole, or the cave. At picnics and parties he was the champion fun maker. Yet such a tragic occurrence had set him to questioning his drifting existence. He began to struggle out of the strong ties binding him to his family and to Hannibal. After two years of it he was growing tired of working without wages for sweet-tempered, ineffective Orion. Slowly he came to a great decision.

Pamela's marriage was one of the factors of his plan. She had known William A. Moffett when he lived in Hannibal and it was during his visit to friends in Hannibal that they became engaged. Moffett was a successful young merchant in St. Louis and took his bride to a comfortable house there. Sam knew that if he went to St. Louis he would be welcome to stay with his sister until he could get a job. Since he was now a skilled compositor, he was confident of getting employment.

When he told all this to his mother, she listened with a face so sad that his resolution was tested to the utmost. But she could not deny that he was right. It was imperative that he begin earning his way. When, on the day of his departure, she had packed his few clothes in a shabby carpetbag, she stood looking at him tenderly. Picking up a copy of the New Testament, she placed his hand on it and made him promise that he would neither drink nor play cards while he was gone. "Write to us, Sam," she pleaded.

It was astonishing to find himself a passenger on the big steamboat which he had so often watched at the wharf or glimpsed from a skiff. As the ship rounded a curve and Hannibal disappeared from sight, the boy was wrenched by a desolating pang. Half-consciously he realized that he was taking leave of boyhood and its magic. Realities stared him in the face. He lifted his head to sniff the wind. A job in St. Louis would merely open a gate to the future. He grinned suddenly and said to himself, "Guess John Robard isn't the only one going off to see the world."

CHAPTER · · · · · · · · FOUR

Although a warm welcome at the Moffetts' greeted the boy from Hannibal, he felt he must be on his own. The day he found a well-paid job as compositor for the *Evening News* he moved to a boardinghouse. Each week he sent money to his mother and then put aside every penny he could spare, for he was determined to make his dream of seeing the world come true.

At Sunday dinner, to which the Moffetts always invited him, he and Pamela joked and teased each other in the same old affectionate way. But after two months had gone by Pamela suddenly criticized her brother's appearance. "Honestly, Sam, you're beginning to look too forlorn. Your coat is so worn it's as shiny as a mirror. Can't you afford to buy

73

a new suit? What are you doing with all your money?"

The question brought a sparkle into Sam's eyes. "Well, Pamela," he answered, in his slow, soft voice, "I intend to get to New York soon as I've saved enough to buy a railroad ticket. That's my first goal."

A few weeks later Sam was on an eastbound train. In his pocket were three silver dollars, and sewed into his jacket was a ten-dollar bill. Before he had spent half his money he had secured employment in New York as compositor for a printing firm. In his free time he explored the city. Although he admired the charming brick houses, surrounded by trees and gardens, on Washington Square, he was most impressed by the Crystal Palace and the massive Croton Reservoir, at the corner of Fifth Avenue and Forty-second Street, then the northern edge of the city. In one of his letters to his mother Sam told about seeing the famous tragedian, Edwin Forrest, in a play called "The Gladiator."

When he had sufficient money in his pocket, Sam went on to Philadelphia, found employment there, and visited such historic places as the grave of Benjamin Franklin and the State House where the Liberty Bell had announced the signing of the Declaration of Independence. He haunted libraries and art galleries and admired the beauty of marble mansions and the majestic stretches of Fairmount Park along the Schuylkill River.

After nearly fifteen months away from home, Sam began longing to return. His principal motive was his anxiety about family affairs. Orion's newspaper had finally collapsed. The sale of the building he had occupied brought just enough to pay his debts. Then this incurable optimist bought, on credit, another paper, in the town of Muscatine, in Iowa, and moved his mother and Henry out there with him.

Of course Henry works without pay, thought Sam in despair. Finally he decided he must return to his family and went by train to St. Louis and there, after a call on Pamela, took a packet boat for Muscatine.

The three members of the Clemens family were at breakfast when he arrived. Their shouts of joy, his mother's embrace, and the incomparable meal set before him, combined to produce a superb welcome. Eagerly Orion said, "Now you'll stay and help me with the paper, won't you?"

Shaking his head, Sam answered that he had to earn real money and was going back to work on the *St. Louis Evening News.* He did so, but after a few months in St. Louis he was again lured to join the family. A major change in the situation had taken place. Orion had impulsively married and once more had moved. This time it was to Keokuk, on the Mississippi River, and there he had set up a printing business.

A happy arrangement had then been made for Mrs. Clemens to accept an oft-repeated invitation from her son-in-law and Pamela to live with them in their roomy house in St. Louis. With her support assured, Sam thought he could afford to join forces with his dearly loved brother

Henry and try to make Orion's business a success. He spent two happy years in Keokuk. But it was impossible to make a profit from any of Orion's enterprises. A restless desire to travel seized upon Sam and he resolved to leave.

Henry unselfishly urged his brother to get away and asked him where he wanted to go. The answer was staggering. Sam had been reading about explorations along the Amazon River in both Peru and Brazil. That was the adventure he would like to join. But first he needed money to get to a town where he could earn some good wages.

Shortly after this secret conversation Sam bolted into the press room one afternoon, triumphantly waving a bit of green paper. "Look what the wind brought me!" he shouted. It was a fifty-dollar bill which had blown against the wall of a store and stuck there long enough to let Sam take a curious look at it. Conscientiously he advertised his find, but days passed without an answer.

"It must have been dropped by a stranger," said Henry. "Anyway, it's yours now. So off you go. What will be your first stop?"

"Cincinnati," replied his brother promptly. "I'll pile up cash there and then go down the river to New Orleans, where I'll get a boat for the Amazon." A few days later he was on his way.

Anyone, like Sam, having his first glimpse of Cincinnati would never have suspected it of emotional undercurrents. Framed in steep hills, it had an air of peaceful prosperity. Passing through the busy traffic up the main street, Sam was impressed with the attractive stores, the churches, the hotels, and a solid-looking bank. On his first day in the town Sam found employment in a printing firm and took up quarters in a cheap boardinghouse. There he shared a room with a Scotchman named MacFarlane, who told him at supper all he knew about Cincinnati.

Early in 1857 this was one of many American towns sharply divided in opinion on national problems. Citizens who followed the debates in Congress which had been going on for twenty years realized that the differences on political, economic, and moral issues between the slave-owning South and the industrial North were bound to reach a culmination soon. Northern congressmen had imposed high tariffs on imports, and these were a burden to Southern planters. On the other hand, Southern legislators had pushed through the Fugitive Slave Law, permitting slave owners to recapture slaves who had escaped to free states. This law aroused to fury Northerners who believed that slavery was a wicked institution which no Christian nation should tolerate. Many of these people might have been justly called fanatics. But the term could also have been applied to Southerners who threatened to withdraw from the Union if slavery was outlawed, because they were convinced that slave labor was essential to the cultivation of the tobacco, cotton, and rice crops on which they depended for their living. Their leaders dreamed of an empire based on slavery which would extend across the southern half of the country from the Atlantic to the Pacific.

Of course there were thousands of Americans who went

about their daily business completely indifferent to the gathering storm. Sam Clemens was one of them. Yet he was startled to learn from MacFarlane that in spite of its leisurely southern aspect, Cincinnati had for years been the home of the Beecher family. In this very town Henry Ward Beecher had preached against slavery from his pulpit, and here his daughter, Harriet Beecher Stowe, had written *Uncle Tom's Cabin*.

MacFarlane agreed with Sam's charge that Harriet Beecher Stowe's novel had done much to fan the flames of sectional emotion, but he did not consider the matter important. He was interested only in philosophy and in other works which interpreted man's existence. "Man was supposed to be the supreme goal of all creation. Instead, he has turned out to be a failure. He alone is capable of sin, crime, and self-destruction."

As he listened, Sam summed up all the instances of greed and selfishness he had observed. He recalled the drunkenness and violence which had sometimes disturbed the peace of Hannibal. MacFarlane's theories would explain such examples of human failure and even Sam's own misdeeds, which always weighed him down with guilt. Neither teacher nor pupil in these nightly classes ever took into consideration the courage, rectitude, and kindness they had certainly found in human beings. His friend's bitter philosophy took deep hold of Sam's soul.

After four months Sam had saved a considerable sum of money. One April day he bade MacFarlane good-by and walked up the gangplank of the *Paul Jones,* bound for New Orleans.

It was a small steamboat, old and battered. Still, Sam found it a luxury to be a passenger. As the boat skirted the Kentucky shore, he leaned over the rail, sniffing the sweet April breeze. Before his second day on board, the old spell of river life took hold of him. He remembered how every one of his old gang had voted that a river pilot's life was his ideal. Now Will Bowen actually was a licensed pilot. Sam recalled how his own envy had struggled with pride in his friend when he heard the news. Piloting wouldn't be as adventurous as exploring the Amazon would be. But suppose that fond dream didn't come true. What would he do next?

To flee from restless thoughts of the future, he climbed up to the pilothouse. He had seen Mr. Horace Bixby only as he passed in and out of the dining saloon, but he knew him by reputation as one of the most skillful pilots on the river. Finding the door of the pilothouse open, Sam stepped across the threshold saying, "Good morning, sir."

Bixby echoed the greeting politely, without turning his head. Sam could see why. He was steering so close to the bank that branches of leaning trees scraped the cabin roof. It was exciting to watch the clever maneuvers. Soon the ship was turned into midstream once more. To his own surprise, Sam heard himself say, "How would you like a young man aboard, to learn the river?"

A piercing glance fixed him for an instant. Then, with

eyes on the course, Bixby answered tersely, "I wouldn't like it. Cub pilots are only trouble."

The swift repulse acted like an electric charge to awaken Sam's old longing. Suddenly he knew he would rather be a pilot than anything else in the world. Seating himself on a bench, he watched the dexterous motions of the man at the wheel and seized every relaxed moment to chat. He observed Bixby's interest upon learning that his visitor came from Hannibal and was a friend of Will Bowen's. Sam let drop the mild boast that, except for a big river steamer, he had steered every kind of boat in every kind of weather on the Mississippi.

Next day he pleased the pilot with praises of his skill. The following morning he entertained him with humorous stories. Every so often he repeated his wish to be taken on as a cub pilot. At last, with a satirical grunt, Bixby said, "Well, let's see. Here, take the wheel. I've got a sore foot. I'll sit down while you steer, and judge whether you've got any sense for it."

Sam felt his heart leap for joy and then instantly sink with fright. Yet it was a glorious sensation to stand there in command. He noted at once that the Ohio's current was far less swift than the Mississippi's. Since little traffic blocked the way and a watchful pilot was beside him, it was sheer bliss to be steering. He was quick to follow Bixby's orders and careful to keep the ship in the current. After this demonstration Bixby allowed him to take the wheel several hours a day while the sore foot was resting. By the time the ship reached the harbor of New Orleans, Sam had made up his mind what to do if his dream of exploration in South America did not materialize.

As soon as the ship docked, he found the proper authority at the shipping office. His question brought a snort of laughter from the clerk. "The Amazon! Young feller, there ain't likely to be a ship headin' there fer maybe a year or so."

To his surprise Sam walked down the wide boulevard with a light heart and a sense of relief. Now he knew what he wanted to do. For an hour he poked about the old city, with its fascinating combination of French and deep South architecture. The two influences seemed typified by a single scene. Along a narrow street flanked by gray brick houses a Negro perched on a pile of cotton bales was driving a two-wheeled cart drawn by a sleepy mule. Above the walled gardens rose pepper trees and palms, half hiding the lacy iron balconies adorned with trailing bougainvillea vines.

Once more aboard the *Paul Jones*, he made a strong plea for Horace Bixby to "teach him the river." For now Sam knew he wanted to be a pilot. For many moments Bixby seemed to be completely absorbed in the last-minute scramble of passengers pushing up the gangplank. Then he turned to scrutinize from head to foot the loose-limbed, slender young man with the thatch of curly red hair.

Next came a cannonade of personal questions. Did Sam Clemens gamble or drink or chew tobacco? A prompt *no* disposed of the queries, one by one. Swearing? "Well," admitted Sam with a grin, "just give me pressure enough, and I'm pretty good at it."

Bixby, who was famous for violent epithets, matched that grin. "All right," he said, "I'll teach you for six hundred dollars. A cub pilot gets room and meals on board, but not a cent for shore leave. How about it?"

Sam was delighted. In a flash he knew how he could jump the financial hurdle. "Mr. Bixby," he answered in his soft drawl, "I want to make piloting my profession. Of course I haven't six hundred dollars at hand. Would you accept this proposition? I'll pay one hundred dollars down and the rest in regular payments when I earn a pilot's salary."

There was a long pause. Bixby finally nodded. "All right. I accept. We'll begin right now. Soon as I pull her out, you can take the boat past all the ships moored here in the harbor." He rang the bell for the engineer. The steam whistle shrieked, and paddle wheels began to turn as the *Paul Jones* backed away from the pier and started to head upstream.

All his life Sam remembered that first lesson. His nervous effort to pass the moored ships brought a contemptuous outburst from his teacher. "Not so far out, you lily-livered coward! Shave those steamboats close as if you were peeling apples. Hug the shore! No, no, not so far in! Here, give me the wheel, you fool!"

In disgrace, the cub stood aside to watch the precision with which the pilot steered within a few inches of each

ship. When they were in the clear, Bixby yielded up the wheel and said pleasantly, "You see, my boy, easy water is close to shore here, and the swift current is outside." Hour by hour instruction was thus served, first with abuse, then with kindness. When the teacher took the wheel he lectured on landings and islands, and pointed out the location of dangerous reefs, sand bars, and snags. The pupil set down all this information in a notebook.

Casually the pilot announced that the whole course would look different on the down trip. "What?" wailed Sam. "You mean to say that the shapes of islands and shores I'm learning now will change?"

Patiently Bixby told him that winds and fluctuation of the water level made many swift changes in the course. Each one had to be noted. "Oh, no!" moaned Sam. "Oh, I haven't the brains for piloting." He was answered by a laugh and a comforting pat on the shoulder.

When at last he was sent to his cabin for the night, he pored over his notes. Next morning he studied maps of the river. He did this whenever he had time off from his duties in the pilothouse. Every moment at the wheel was exciting, but often he despaired of making progress.

Of course the worst strain came on the night shift, especially in fog and rain. In this era, long before Thomas Edison harnessed electricity to man's use, boats had no searchlights. Nor was there a single buoy or lighthouse to point the way. As he peered into the blackness ahead Sam shivered with terror to think that the safety of ship, passengers, and cargo hung perilously on the pilot's skill and judgment. Could he ever acquire the confidence to handle a ship all alone?

Never had he imagined so exacting a job. It was fascinating to watch Bixby force the ship over a sand bar or cross the mile-wide river at just the right point for resisting the fierce current. It would be long before he could match such skill. Yet he was beginning to know what the *Paul Jones* could do. He was getting acquainted with the personality of the river. As he stood beside Bixby, watching him maneuver the boat along the crowded water front of St.

Louis, and glanced at the levee crowded with carts and drays, Sam felt the intoxicating foretaste of a glorious future.

In this mood of triumph he burst in upon his sister and mother. They listened eagerly to the story of his experiences and heartily approved his choice of vocation. Will Moffett approved also. He willingly loaned his brother-in-law the first payment due his teacher.

In high spirits Sam returned to the ship. Horace Bixby greeted him pleasantly, but his manner held a forewarning of the trials awaiting Sam.

As they continued up the river Sam became sharply aware of a pilot's dependence on soundings. With the ears of a hawk he listened to the leadman's droning song as the lead was lowered to the bottom. Exact information was needed as the ship was guided through a channel between shore and islands or around the dangerous shoals that were encountered whenever the ship crossed to the opposite side of the river. Solemn and slow came the chant. "Mark seven." "Deep four." "Quarter less three." "Mark twain." The numbers referred to fathoms, and each fathom measured six feet. Since the *Paul Jones* drew nine feet, the signal "Mark twain," meaning a depth of about twelve feet, warned that possible shallow water might lie ahead.

Not only did a pilot have to be guided by soundings, he must fix in his memory some shore point by which he could tell that safe water could be assured on the return trip.

Bixby, who recognized the slightest change in the known course, could go ahead confidently. The novice found the double effort an intolerable strain.

"Jumping Jehoshaphat!" he would moan. "If I could remember where all those points and shoals and snags are for a thousand miles, I'd be able to raise the dead. And then I wouldn't be piloting a steamboat."

"Stop that!" Bixby growled. "When I say I'll learn a man the river, I mean it!"

After weeks of intensive instruction Sam was allowed to steer all by himself while the pilot took a nap. Although he knew he was trusted this way only during the safest portion of the course he was very proud to be in sole charge. Apparently noting this state of self-satisfaction, Bixby sprang a surprise test. After announcing that he was going below he rehearsed Sam on the course. The pupil had it by heart: inside the first snag above the point, outside the next one, start out from the lower end of Higgins' wood-yard and make a square crossing. Bixby nodded and said he'd be back by the end of that run.

Happy and secure in his knowledge, Sam covered the course. Bixby did not return just then, but the young man at the wheel was confident. Then . . . . Horrors! A reef loomed up straight ahead. In panic he whirled the wheel. But although the ship spun around, the reef still seemed to lie almost under the bow. Sam rang frantic signals to the engineer. In response the ship first backed, next tore ahead, then headed straight for the trees along the shore.

At this moment Bixby strolled in and quietly gave directions which put the boat back on course. After a few sarcastic questions, he remarked that the reef which had aroused such fright in Sam was merely a stretch of ruffled water. Yes, he admitted, it did look like the real thing, but it was only a wind reef. Thereupon he ordered Sam to steer the ship over it. After one amazed glare, Sam prepared himself for a crash which would wreck the ship and kill everyone in it. Then he obeyed. A soft ripple of water was all that struck the bow.

Sam wiped the perspiration from his brow. "How in the name of great Caesar's ghost am I going to tell a wind reef?"

"Oh, by instinct," was the offhand reply. "You'll just get to know it from a reef."

Months later Sam failed a far more tricky test in so sensational a fashion that the episode became a legend among river men. Once again Bixby simply left the pilothouse with a wave of the hand to his pupil, stopping in the doorway to ask, "You know how much water is in the next crossing?"

"Why, sir, it's practically bottomless here. 'Course I know!"

With a shrug, the pilot murmured, "Oh, you think so, do you?" and disappeared.

His tone alarmed Sam. Had the crazy river changed that much? Soon he was aware that the captain and the mate were standing below on the hurricane deck, looking uneasy. A clerk and one passenger after another joined the group to stare ahead in obvious disquiet. Suddenly the captain asked loudly where Mr. Bixby was and then shouted an order for the leadmen to take soundings. By that time consternation had taken possession of Sam. He was certain he saw shoals ahead. When the mournful chant from the leadmen floated to his ears, telling of ever shallower water, he was in a panic. Violently ringing signals to the engineer, he sent the ship first to port, then to starboard. Every move seemed to bring her nearer to danger than the last. His trembling hands could hardly hold the wheel. At last he seized the speaking tube and shouted, "Oh, Ben, if you love me, back her! Quick, Ben! Oh, back the immortal soul out of her!"

A second later he saw that Mr. Bixby was standing there smiling at him. A roar of laughter rose from the crowd below. Sam realized now that he had been the victim of a plot. There never had been any danger. The course was as safe as a quiet harbor. Fury welled up in him at such a betrayal. With iron control, he put the ship on the proper marks and signaled the engineer to send her ahead. Looking over his shoulder, he said bitterly, "A fine trick!"

Bixby said quietly, "Didn't you know there was no bottom in this crossing?"

"Yes, sir, I did."

"Very well. Let nobody shake your confidence in your own firm knowledge. That's what I wanted you to realize. If you stand by what you know you won't be fooled."

Sam said nothing. It took all his will power to keep down his rage. Later, however, he admitted he had received a lesson he would never forget. He could profit by it. If only the men wouldn't mock his wild call to Ben, the engineer! But of course that was just what they did. Sam's only comfort was that with the passage of time Horace Bixby not only trusted him more, but gradually became his warm friend.

It was a blow to Sam when his chief was transferred to another post. There was need of a highly skilled man to manage traffic on the Missouri River, for hundreds of people were now westward bound. Not only had silver been found in Nevada, luring men to a new search for treasure, but the Oregon Trail had been opened up by Dr. Marcus Whitman and his wife Narcissa, and whole families of settlers were moving out to the great Northwest.

Sam Clemens was transferred to the *John Roe*, an easygoing freighter with an easygoing pilot. Usually the families of some of the owners were on board, and they made the voyage gay with parties. Often Sam joined the dancing and sometimes he was persuaded to sing old ballads and strum accompaniments on the ship's piano. He spent much of his spare time in reading.

Then came a transfer to a magnificent new ship, the *Pennsylvania*. At first he was jubilant, but he soon discovered that the pilot, although skillful at the wheel, was an ignorant, envious tyrant, impossible to please. He took delight in making his assistant's life miserable.

During a stopover at St. Louis Sam exploded to the Moffetts, his mother, and Henry, who was now living with them. "Hardest of all," he told them, "is that no matter how he roars at me, bullies me, and finds fault, I have to be polite and submissive. It's as much as I can do to hold my temper. Every night before I go to sleep I kill Pilot Brown in a different fashion. He really is an old devil."

The next time he stopped at St. Louis Sam begged Henry to take the trip down to New Orleans with him. "You'll just have to do a bit of work, nothing much, to pay your passage," he explained. "We can both earn some pocket money by guarding the freight at night on the docks where the ship ties up."

Henry, who was only doing odd jobs at a printing firm, was delighted with the idea. He and his brother always had a good time together. Besides, in no time the charming, lively boy made friends with everyone on the ship—except, of course, the pilot. He glowered at both the Clemens boys when Sam was at the wheel. Henry's pride in Sam's knowledge of the river and his skill was all too evident to the mean-minded man.

But his rudeness could be shrugged off by two boys who were otherwise enjoying themselves to the full. Henry was persuaded to take another trip on the *Pennsylvania*. One day, however, Mr. Brown grew so angry at some innocent remark of Henry's that he struck him in the face, calling him a vile name. Sam's pent-up hatred of his boss was instantly unloosed; he knocked Brown flat and pummeled

him as hard as he could, before concern for the ship made him stop. He jumped to the wheel and took over until the pilot scrambled to his feet and seized the wheel himself.

News of the row swept over the ship. Sam's unpardonable act delighted officers, crew, and passengers. Of course the captain had an interview with the cub pilot, but instead of putting him in irons, as Brown had fully expected, the captain had to make an effort not to laugh heartily at his account of the affair. When the pilot refused to allow his assistant in the pilothouse again, the captain wanted to discharge the man. But he could not fill his place until they returned to St. Louis. It was arranged to give Sam a pass on the *Lacey*, which left New Orleans two days later. Henry was to remain on the *Pennsylvania*.

Sam bade his brother good-by and added, "Don't go near the old devil. We'll get a decent pilot at St. Louis. I'll see you there."

As a passenger Sam had time to make up sleep. But when the *Lacey* stopped at Greenville, he went up on deck. As he leaned over the rail a man came running down the wharf and shouted, "The *Pennsylvania's* blown up! Just below Memphis! More'n a hundred people killed!"

As horror-stricken passengers milled around the deck, shouting at the man who had brought the news, demanding that the captain tell them if it was true, some of them saw a red-haired youth stagger from the rail as if he had been shot. One man, who flung out an arm to support him, heard him moaning, "Henry! Henry!"

For two endless days Sam walked the deck in anguish. His despair was so complete that he found it impossible to hope that his beloved younger brother had escaped. When at last he landed in Memphis, Sam found Henry in an improvised hospital filled with victims of the accident. The boy was conscious; he tried to smile and said that Sam was not to worry. A volunteer nurse with a tray of medicines in her hand stopped long enough to take Sam aside for a brief talk. She told Sam that his brother, who had tried to save other passengers, had been so badly burned that there was little hope of recovery. With a leaden heart, Sam left that grim place of suffering to send Orion a telegram. Then he hurried back to sit beside the mattress where Henry lay. Doctors and nurses paid the boy special attention, but they could do little. Sam kept a ceaseless vigil, to make sure he would be there whenever his brother opened his eyes and smiled. Henry lived only two days. Orion, arriving just after his death, found Sam in a state of hysterical grief. "The light of my life has gone out!" he kept sobbing.

To his heartbroken mother Sam insisted that it was all his fault. He had persuaded Henry to travel on that ill-fated ship. He should have been with him, somehow managed to protect him. So violent was his sorrow and his self-blame that his mother had to put aside her own grief to calm and comfort him.

Fortunately for his sanity, Sam had to return to the exacting duties of his job as pilot. There was healing in the ceaseless concentration it demanded. In August, 1858, he was granted his pilot's license, an achievement he reached in the short period of eighteen months.

During the next three years Sam was supremely satisfied with his job as a pilot. Many were his picturesque adventures and many were the friends he made. His salary was princely for that era. Even though he sent money to his mother and to the unfortunate Orion he was able to save a great deal.

River life was an absorbing, satisfying existence. And the king of it was the pilot. All the pilots were members of an association and had clubrooms in New Orleans, where they met to swap stories and share news of the latest tricks played by the Mississippi. They joked and teased one another with the freedom of royal equals. Sam was a favorite at these sessions because of the amusing way he could tell tall stories.

Even when the year 1860 was drawing to a close, these young men hardly ever discussed the state of the nation. They were so detached from other phases of life that they could dismiss the amazing episode of John Brown's raid on Harpers Ferry with the contemptuous phrase, "The poor old man was certainly crazy!"

As individuals, however, they must have followed events with some concern. In November of that year Abraham Lincoln was elected president. A few weeks later South Carolina seceded from the Union. Early in February,

1861, seven more Southern states seceded and formed the Confederated States of America. At dawn, April 12, Fort Sumter, a Federal fort at the entrance to Charleston harbor, was bombarded by South Carolina cannon, and three days later President Lincoln called for seventy-five thousand volunteers to defend the Union.

At ease in their clubrooms, the river pilots discussed the possibility of war. Some of them thought the dark clouds would blow over. Others declared comfortably that if there was fighting, it certainly wouldn't last.

One evening while his ship was docked for the night, Pilot Samuel Clemens dressed himself in a new suit. With a winged shirt collar peeping over a black satin stock, and sideburns framing his cheeks, he was the very personification of style. The occasion for which he had prepared was dinner with his old chief, Horace Bixby. They met at the most famous Creole restaurant in New Orleans and exchanged recollections. "Do you remember the time. . . ." Sam would begin, and Bixby, chuckling with amusement, would tell the anecdote from his point of view. It was a delightful evening.

A few days later Sam had a startling message from his friend. It brought his first shock of recognition that something truly serious was happening to the country. Horace Bixby had joined the United States River Service and was to go on duty for the Union up the Missouri River. This surprising decision aroused Sam's slumbering consciousness of the rift opening between men, between whole regions. It served as a slight preparation for the violent manner in which only a little later Sam Clemens was to encounter the Civil War.

CHAPTER · · · · · · · FIVE

Late that same spring Pilot Clemens was traveling as a passenger on the *Uncle Sam*, bound for St. Louis, where a new assignment was waiting for him. At New Orleans he was pleased to find that the ship's pilot was an old friend, called Zeb. At once Sam was invited to share his watch and the two young men passed untroubled hours in high spirits.

As the *Uncle Sam* neared the Cairo wharf, Sam turned from the pilothouse window to cry, "Look, Zeb, there are a lot of men drilling in a field. Wonder if they're getting ready to go gunning for the Yanks." A shrug and a laugh were the pilot's response.

At Memphis the local feelings were more definitely expressed. There on the bluffs a gang of Negroes, directed by men wearing caps of Confederate gray, were hard at work. Some of them urged mules to drag cannons into position. Others were themselves placing batteries at the bluff's edge.

Turning to the captain at the ship's rail, Sam said, "Looks as if these people meant to blockade the river, doesn't it, sir?"

The captain snorted. "They can no more blockade this river than they can tame it!" With that he walked off to laugh away the fears of the passengers massed on deck.

The approach to St. Louis always stirred a hundred recollections in Sam's mind. How many, many times he had steered ships over these waters! Hanging out of the pilothouse window, he remarked to Zeb, "There's the ugly old Jefferson Barracks coming on the—"

His last word was clipped by the roar of cannon. Smoke engulfed the ship. Two pairs of startled eyes saw a cannon ball hit the water a few yards off the ship's bow. "Good glory!" yelled Zeb. "Is this target practice?"

With a quick twist of the wheel, he steered the steamer out from shore. A second deafening explosion was followed by a crash of glass, as the shattered windows of the pilothouse fell to the floor. Zeb fell, too, shouting, "What on earth does this mean?"

Sam had sprung to the wheel and was steering it around in a circle to face back to shore. "Guess they want us to stop and see them," he explained calmly. Never before had he made so swift a landing as at the wharf of that barracks.

Frightened passengers had rushed on deck. The captain ordered a gangplank lowered and stood at the head of it, glaring down at three men in the uniform of the United States Army. "What do you think you're doing, firing on a passenger ship?" he roared.

"Sorry, sir!" replied the first officer, firmly walking up the gangplank. "We have orders to search all ships. Your pilot didn't stop on signal. Please let me see your papers, Captain."

With a grunt of rage the captain took the man to his cabin. The second officer gave a command to his companion. "Better go below and check the cargo for guns and ammunition." The examination took only ten minutes. Formally saluting the captain, the chief officer said, "All clear! We're still letting commercial ships go through." The three soldiers then went ashore.

With Sam and Zeb, the captain stood gazing ruefully at the glass and plaster on the pilothouse floor. "Looks like river travel isn't going to be a picnic from now on."

Sam was the first on shore. He strode to the steamship headquarters to learn the truth about the situation. "Is the ship I'm engaged to pilot sailing tomorrow?" he asked. "Not likely," he was told. "We're waiting to hear. Probably all river traffic is going to be stopped. We'll let you know."

Could this really be his last trip on the Mississippi as a

pilot? Forlornly Sam walked toward the Moffetts' house. Already the town had changed. People were sauntering dejectedly along the streets. Many stores had hung out the Stars and Stripes. Suddenly a passer-by stopped to shake his fist at the flag. Instantly a crowd gathered around him and there arose a din of angry voices. Sam walked on in bewilderment. Is everybody taking sides in this fuss, he wondered. From all he had heard and read in the journals, Missouri was about as divided as Kansas. Look at his own family: his mother a typical Southerner; Orion an abolitionist; the Moffetts, puzzled neutrals. Of course they differed peaceably. But suppose things came to real fighting! It was with a heavy heart that he greeted the family so eagerly waiting for him.

Next day Sam learned that no steamships were going south on the river. So now what was he going to do? To ease his restless gloom he decided after a few days of misery to go up to Hannibal and hear what his friends had to say. A warm welcome greeted him in the old town from practically everyone he met on the streets or in the homes he knew so well. All the young fellows were forming companies to drill in open meadows and camp in the woods. Sam was invited to join several of these groups. "Which side are you on?" he would ask. Often the answer was evasive. "We ain't decided yet, but we've got a good camp. Come and see it."

Will Bowen, however, was outspoken. During supper at his home he told his old chum that he was forming a company to defend Missouri against invasion. "For a while," he said, "I didn't know where I belonged. Then I decided to copy General Robert E. Lee. Lee had to defend Virginia and I'm for my state. Maybe I'll join the Confederate Army. Our outfit is going on an expedition in a couple of days. Better come along."

To fight for peace in one's own state sounded to Sam like a possible position to take. Why agonize about a tempest that might blow over? The moment he reached the camp where Will's battalion was drilling he tossed off serious speculations. Bear Creek was the very place where the pirates used to meet. Around the campfire were many of the same old gang, dreaming of glory in the same old way. The air was filled with song and laughter and boasting. They meant to chase the Yanks out of the region. Not a Yank would live to tell the tale.

On the night of departure the volunteers were very solemn. Their destination was unknown, but they expected to do battle and each went to bid his girl a tender and sorrowful farewell. An hour later they were marching four abreast through dark woodland paths. First they headed for another county, to be sworn in by a Confederate colonel. The officer gave them breakfast and sent them off with two notes of commendation. One was to the commander of an enlisting station some miles away, and the other to a farmer pledged to help the Southern cause. He made his promise good by providing horses and camp gear.

Next morning, when the spoils were divided, Sam found

himself on a mule with a tasseled tail. His garb consisted
of a big felt hat, high boots, a sword, and a suit half covered with a blanket roll. Somehow he managed to drape
on the saddle all he had brought from home, an overcoat,
a quilt, and a tin pail for coffee. Over his shoulder he carried a gun. The resulting combination of cowboy, camper,
and soldier brought shouts of laughter from his companions.

No one laughed harder than Sam. Instinctively he knew
that the whole enterprise was play-acting. At first everyone
took comedy parts and enjoyed them. But with no real direction, the battalion's long, tiresome treks brought it no
nearer action. Its elected officers were mere pals, whose authority carried no weight. As the troop moved here and
there with no definite purpose, the war proved increasingly
disappointing, and the bored heroes did nothing but growl
and curse the day they had tried to get into it.

Second Lieutenant Samuel L. Clemens was the envy of
all. He managed to break his ankle, could neither ride nor
walk, and was the petted guest of a farm family devoted
to the Confederate cause. Now and then Union scouts
would search the house for Rebs, and the farmer's wife
would hide her "wounded" soldier under mountains of
bedcovers.

Between such rare moments of excitement Sam read the
few books possessed by the family and reflected on his
future. He was convinced that soldiering was not for him.
It was becoming plain that Missouri would be dominated

by Union troops and sympathizers. Orion, an impassioned abolitionist, offered the best possibility of safety to his ex-Confederate-soldier brother. But would he forgive him for having taken up—though briefly—that hated cause? There was nothing to do but find out. As soon as he could walk without too much pain, Sam set forth on foot for Keokuk, journeying stealthily at night.

To his amazement Orion not only gave him the warmest possible welcome, but expressed only mild reproof for the witless escapade with Will Bowen's crowd. Moreover, he had wonderful news to relate. His old St. Louis friend, Mr. Edward Bates, the distinguished lawyer, had been appointed Attorney General by President Lincoln, and as a member of the Cabinet had considerable influence. When a politician named James W. Nye was made Governor of the Territory of Nevada, Bates secured for Orion Clemens an appointment as Territorial Secretary, with a salary of $1800 a year.

As he watched the stunning effect of this report upon his successful pilot brother, Orion's grave, handsome face expressed unwonted triumph. He was pleased when Sam slapped him on the back and exclaimed, "Good for you! This is great, Orion."

Actually, however, the news had aroused in Sam something he had never felt before, a bitter envy. Ever since those first caravans had stopped in Hannibal on their way west, he had cherished a smothered longing to see that part of the country. Lately the popular attention given to California had switched to Nevada after discovery of gold and silver there. The rush of treasure hunters to the region almost equaled that of the forty-niners. And here was Orion, of all people, having the luck to be sent out there! The contrast with his own situation—no job, no plan, no future—chilled him to the bone.

Through his black mood and his shame for feeling envy, Orion's hesitating voice penetrated. "I confess, Sam, that there's one big problem to be solved before I can accept this position. I can't get an advance on my salary, and the government won't pay my way out there. I . . . I've been wondering, Sam, if . . . if you could afford to pay for both of us, and consider acting as my secretary."

Sam did not turn around, lest the ray of hope just offered would fade. "It would be fine to have you," Orion went on. "I'm afraid you'd get no salary. But"—here the voice rose to its familiar tone of optimism—"why couldn't we stake a mining claim and make our fortunes? Big ones have been made in Nevada. Would you consider this proposal?"

Would he consider it! Sam had to exert his will power to keep from dancing a jig. But he managed an unhurried reply. He said that since the river was closed to regular traffic and he had made a botch of soldiering, he might as well take a chance on mining. "I've got plenty of money to get us out there and settled," he concluded.

Turning at last to see Orion's radiant face, he cut short his brother's attempted expression of gratitude by asking, "How soon can we start for Nevada?"

Plans had all been considered. Molly was to stay with

her parents in Keokuk until her husband could afford to
have her come west. She would attend to moving their
possessions. Sam and his brother had only to get their official credentials and pack up. They had to take the Missouri River boat at St. Louis. Before the week was out, the
brothers were waving good-by to their mother and the
Moffetts from the deck of a small steamer bound for St.
Joseph, on the western border of Missouri.

The six-day voyage was a trial to the former Mississippi
pilot. His talent for picturesque swearing was in constant
use to express his contempt for the shallow, snag-filled
river, the slow vessel, and the dull scenery. When they
reached St. Joseph, they went at once to the office of the
Overland Stagecoach Company to buy their tickets. Orion
groaned at the price. "One hundred and fifty dollars apiece
is a good deal more than I thought it would be," he muttered apologetically.

Sam reminded him of the far worse alternatives. Either
they would have to voyage all the way around South
America or make the tiresome crossing of the Isthmus of
Panama before boarding a ship for San Francisco. No railroad went farther west than Chicago. The mighty project
to span the continent by the Union Pacific Railroad was
only in the planning stage. "I think," he said, "we ought
to be mighty grateful that this coach company was finally
started."

The restrictions on luggage, however, were dismaying.
When they asked an official how to get their trunks over

the river to the coach, he roared, "Trunks! Merciful heavens, boys, send 'em back where they came from. You can carry twenty-five pounds apiece and no more."

Orion was aghast. Since he absolutely had to take a huge bundle of government statutes applicable to territories, and since he refused to give up his unabridged dictionary, he had only fifteen pounds left for clothes. The only way out was to wear their heaviest suits, shirts, and boots, then carefully select forty pounds of garments and pack discards into the trunks for shipping back to Keokuk.

Early in the morning of July 26, 1861, the Territorial Secretary and his secretary crossed the river into Kansas. With deep interest they studied the waiting coach. It was a great handsome affair slung on iron springs. The six horses that would pull it were being backed into place. The two young men were disturbed to see quantities of huge mailbags and bundles inside the coach, as well as piled on top. There was only room for one long bench in the rear.

With a pitying shake of the head, the conductor announced, "We're carrying three days' delayed mail. Lucky we've got only one passenger besides you two."

Mr. George Bemis, the fellow passenger, came up to introduce himself. He advised filling canteens with water and keeping blankets ready for the sharp air of the mountain regions. All three settled themselves on the rear bench. The conductor swung up on the outside seat, beside the driver, who cracked his long whip. The horses plunged into a gallop and the coach, swinging and swaying, rolled off at a gallant pace. As he hung out of the window to revel in the fresh, sunny morning, Sam tingled with a glorious sense of freedom and adventure.

Every ten miles the coach stopped to change horses at one of the company's way stations. This was accomplished with lightning speed. After a while the gently rolling Kansas country became a level plain gold with wheat as far as eye could see. At noon and at sunset the five men were given simple meals at the stations. Then on they went through the night.

It was not yet dawn on the second day of travel when Sam felt something give way underneath the coach floor. The horses were jerked to a stop and both conductor and driver poked about with lanterns. After a period of growling together, they yelled to the passengers to get out. They had found a bad break in the huge leather belt, or thorough brace, which held the springs.

"Comes of having to carry three days' mail!" groaned the conductor. "And right here we're going to unload it. We'll send a guard to pick it up tomorrow."

With the aid of the passengers all the bags were heaved from the roof and about half the mail and packages were hauled from inside the coach. They all lay at the roadside in a mountainous heap, to take rain or sun as chance determined.

"Now look!" said the conductor as the passengers were about to climb inside again. "I've covered the entire floor with the mailbags that are left. Just spread your blankets on top of them and you can stretch out and be twice as comfortable."

It was true. When the thorough brace was mended and the coach sped on again, it swayed like a cradle and the passengers, horizontal and relaxed, fell into a blissful sleep. It was disturbed only when the unabridged dictionary was jarred out of place and hit an elbow or an unsuspecting nose.

During the day the most exciting moment was arrival at a station. Loud and clear the conductor blew his horn. The driver urged his horses into a last spurt and with a clatter of horses' hoofs, the stage whirled up to the group of adobe houses and stopped. The hostlers, the handy men, and the cook sprang out with whoops of welcome. All attention was concentrated on the driver, king of the road. The conductor was met with cool nods and the passengers were practically overlooked. Meals, served on greasy tables, were almost impossible to eat. A hunk of bread and sometimes a bit of fruit kept the travelers alive.

Three hundred miles from St. Joseph the coach crossed the Platte River, and now the wild life of the plains became increasingly fascinating. Jack rabbits of enormous size, hungry-looking coyotes that could run at incredible speed, now and then a graceful antelope, occasionally a wolf— all made their appearance. On the fifth day of the journey the coach reached Julesburg on the South Platte River at the far eastern corner of what is now Colorado. It seemed odd to be in a town again and see stores, saloons, two hotels, and a post office. At Julesburg coaches were always replaced by smaller covered conveyances called mud wagons. They were supposed to be stout enough to stand rough going across creek beds and mountain ridges.

But this party's mud wagon broke down after a few miles, and to repair it required several hours. These hours were well spent, however, for a hunting party had gathered at the coach station and the three passengers were invited to join it and were provided with horses. This was a buffalo hunt. Sam had never seen a buffalo, and when the party came upon a small herd grazing in a hollow, he reined in his horse, to stare. It amazed him to observe how the buffalo's bulk is concentrated in his deep chest and huge, horned head, decorated by a beard. The hindquarters look weak in comparison and the hoofs seem positively dainty. Nevertheless the small feet galloped off too fast for the hunters to get a single shot at their prey.

Next day came another interesting encounter. About noon the driver called back to his passengers, "You fellows watch sharp now. Along about here's where we most often meet the pony express."

Sam let out a whoop of joy. He had been hoping to lay eyes upon it. Thus far the riders had always passed the stagecoach at night. The conductor had given Sam all the details about this extraordinary service by which mail between St. Joseph, Missouri, and Sacramento, California, was delivered in eight days. It was maintained by eighty riders and four hundred horses. Day after day in each di-

rection the nineteen hundred miles were covered by means of the world's longest relay race—a race against time, against the weather, and often against hostile Indians.

"Here he comes!" yelled the conductor.

A speck in the distance; a horse and rider plainly seen; now life-size; now passing with a hand waved to acknowledge cheers from the wagon, then gone; again a mere dot swiftly vanishing in the dust. It was a breath-taking sight.

"He was so small and thin!" gasped Orion. "Are they all like that?"

"Yep," answered the conductor, "and they dress light even in winter. Did you notice how little and flat the mail pouches were? Only important stuff goes by express—mostly business. Each letter costs five dollars."

Sam mused upon this heroic enterprise. In imagination he followed the riders at night as they pushed through the heavy desert sands or struggled up steep, snowy mountain trails. How long would it be, he wondered, before the picturesque pony express was supplanted by railroads, so clearly destined to spin webs of steel across the great West.

After the coach had passed Fort Laramie, in the southeast portion of the region which became Wyoming twenty-nine years later, it entered the danger zone of hostile Indians. All day the passengers were cautioned to keep the curtains over the windows. At night, with guns ready, they joined the watch. Although he spoke lightly of his many escapes from death, the driver had pulled up his trouser leg to exhibit the jagged scar left from a bullet wound, a convincing proof of peril.

"Don't forgit, though," remarked the conductor comfortingly, "that we got it safe and easy in a fast-moving mud wagon compared to them boys that run mountain-coach stations."

Already he had described the triple threat they faced. Not only were Indians or roaming mountain men likely to raid the stations, but all too often there were outbreaks among the employees. Only men of rough and reckless character would work in these lonely sections. Many of them were criminals wanted for murder or robbery.

The best-known station supervisor was a man named Slade, who had become famous as utterly fearless, quick on the trigger, and a matchless marksman. The Overland Coach Company employed him to conquer trouble wherever it broke out. He could bring order to the most unruly station, stop thieving and fighting, and keep coaches running on time. His technique was simple. Anyone loafing on the job, disobeying orders, or disrupting the service was promptly shot or hung. Naturally, as tradition had it, this man was equally severe with his personal enemies. For hours the conductor regaled his passengers with tales of Slade's ruthless acts of vengeance.

For two days and nights the mud wagon was pulled slowly uphill. The air was cool and fresh and the landscape grew magnificent, with forests sweeping up toward purple peaks. On the third morning, just after dawn, they stopped at a station for breakfast and found it crowded with ranchmen, mountaineers, and company employees on their way to new assignments. At the table taken by the five new arrivals from the mud wagon the one remaining empty seat was soon filled.

A tall man, well dressed in riding clothes, approached with a pleasant smile for all and seated himself beside Sam. As he courteously asked the driver about his trip, Sam noted his excellent English and pleasing voice. His table manners were faultless. It was very odd to encounter an educated gentleman in such a remote spot.

The wagon driver, always first to finish a meal, waved a hand in salute to this man on his way out, and said, "Well, good luck to you, Slade!"

Slade! Sam's start almost upset his coffee cup. Here beside him, serenely eating his breakfast, was the legendary monster with twenty-six murders to his credit. Sam's quick glance imprinted for all time on his memory that triangular, sunburned face, with its broad forehead and thin, malicious mouth. What luck, he thought, to have had such a close view of this celebrated character.

From that morning onward the scenic magnificence of the country increased mile by mile. First came the marvel of seeing snow in August. Crowned in dazzling white at noon, glowing at sunrise and sunset, rose mighty peaks. Hour by hour Sam watched them in complete absorption. Here was beauty and glory. Never before had he been so stirred by the majesty of creation.

At a cleared spot above the tree line the driver stopped his horses, and said, "Here we are at the Great Divide! Git out and I'll show you a sample of what explorers call the continental watershed."

Tramping through thick undergrowth, the travelers were guided to a stream which separated itself into two smaller streams. "This one at the left," said the driver, "is startin' west to the Pacific Ocean. The other one aims to join the Mississippi and reach the Gulf."

For a long time after the wagon started on its way Sam traced in imagination the course of that eastbound stream. Through woods and around rocks it wound its way, joining small rivers here and there, until it reached the Father of Waters, and at last its goal.

The long, long descent into the valley gave extraordinary views of storms and sunshine, of weird rocky shapes and stretches of level plain far below. Although they knew in advance that they were approaching Salt Lake City, their arrival brought a surprise to Sam and his brother. Wide, clean streets and attractive shops and homes gave the town an unexpected air of civilization. At the hotel they had a good scrub in hot water before partaking of an excellent dinner. Their two days of luxury seemed all too short. With the feeling of visitors to a foreign land they walked the length and breadth of the Mormon settlement, staring curiously at the citizens who, so incredibly, looked just like the folks at home.

Following the conductor's advice, all three passengers filled their canteens before they left Salt Lake City and provided themselves with enough food to last the next sixty-eight miles of dreary alkali desert. The sweating mules plowed at a snail's pace through the salty dust, with only one stop between stations for water, which had to be brought to this arid region in barrels. Under the blistering sun, the empty stretches revealed no sign of life, no growing thing but gray sagebrush. To climb to the high mountainous region of Nevada was an inexpressible relief, but a short one. Another huge desert had to be crossed. Along the entire way were strewn the bones of cattle and horses, wagon wheels, and the remains of wrecked carts—pitiful testimony to the disasters befalling early emigrants to California.

One morning, when Sam turned from the window to

awaken his sleeping brother, he said, "This is the twentieth
day since we started from St. Jo. Maybe it's our last morning in the wagon."

Orion was not so sure. But at about noon the driver,
pointing straight ahead, suddenly shouted, "There you
are, boys!" With straining eyes the passengers made out
through the chalky dust something that looked like a handful of sugar lumps tossed down at the foot of towering
mountains. "That's Carson City," said the driver, "capital
of the territory of Nevada."

A few miles farther on the outline of a town grew clear,
and the Territorial Secretary gathered up his collection of
statutes and piled them on the big dictionary, wearing a
look of happy excitement. But Sam did not share his pleasure. "Shucks," he moaned, "I hate to have this trip end.
These have been the most wonderful twenty days I ever
spent."

CHAPTER · · · · · · · SIX

Carson City was a large collection of flimsy cottages, a human huddle on the border of a vast plain walled in by gigantic mountains. Dismounting from the mud wagon, when it stopped in the middle of the town, the passengers found themselves on the edge of a wide circle lined with stores and saloons. This was called the plaza. Orion and Sam bade good-by to Mr. George Bemis, the driver, and the conductor, and set off to find rooms.

An hour later they were settling themselves in a boardinghouse kept by a pleasant Irishwoman. On the second floor Sam secured a cot in a long room occupied by fourteen young men who called themselves the Brigade. They claimed to be friends of Governor James W. Nye and had followed him to the West in the hope of securing political posts. Orion had a bedroom to himself, but he had to use it also as his office.

From the first moment in town Sam yielded completely to the spell of pioneer life. To avoid looking like an outsider, he had adopted an extremely informal costume. He wore wrinkled pants never quite tucked into his boots, a blue woolen shirt always hanging out over his belt somewhere, a shapeless felt hat on his unkempt, bushy hair, and never a coat or vest.

Orion was appalled by his secretary's appearance. "To think," he mourned, "what a dandy you were only a few months ago, as a pilot. It's shameful, the way you look."

Sam laughed, and replied that his attire was in keeping with Nevada's complete freedom. Since his secretarial labors were nonexistent, Sam could amuse himself all day by slouching against the wall of some store to watch what went on in the plaza. Furiously galloping miners, ranchers, mountaineers, and travelers offered a constant exhibit of superb horsemanship. Almost every day a dramatic quarrel took place, with furious words and waving pistols. Several times a week nature put on a show in the early afternoon. From Washoe County in western Nevada came a wild wind named for its place of origin, blowing away everything not firmly attached. Clutching his hat with one hand and holding on to a railing with the other, Sam watched pails, boxes, and even roofs go sailing into the air. When the gale ceased the whole town was covered with white dust.

After some weeks a young Easterner on vacation, who had taken a fancy to Sam, persuaded him to go on a walking trip to famous Lake Tahoe. It meant trudging mile after mile up one mountain and down another, but fatigue was forgotten the instant the pair caught sight of the lake. Six thousand feet above sea level, surrounded by lofty forests, the dazzling blue, crystal-clear water mirrored the grandeur of earth and sky.

When the young men found an unoccupied camp, Sam, reverting to the practices of his pirate gang, gleefully borrowed a coffeepot and a canoe. As he and his friend paddled over the still water, they could look down through thirty feet of liquid blue. Camping on shore was a matchless experience of bright days and starlit nights in the pine-scented air. Their meals consisted only of the fish they caught and the dry bread they had carried with them, but this was a small deprivation compared to such riches.

Sam returned to Carson City just in time for the meeting of the Territorial Legislature. During the sixty-day session he was a frequent visitor, and his keen eyes and ears missed nothing. With scorn he watched the representatives spitting tobacco juice on the floor and lounging with feet on desks. At the close of the last session Sam stood at the back of the assembly room to admire the Secretary's cordial way of shaking hands with many of the members as they walked out. Then he and his brother stood side by side under the portico to enjoy the lively scene of departure.

"A fine collection of legislators," drawled Sam, "especially the man from Washoe County. He can spit the farthest."

It was some time later when Sam Clemens at last caught the treasure-hunting fever. His long indifference to it had made him a marked man. There was only one general topic in Carson City—the mineral wealth hidden in the mountains. Just let a hint drop that a new silver lode had been found on some mountain, and the value of a staked claim on that mountain would shoot skyward. Two months after Sam and his brother arrived, a new vein of silver was opened up in an almost abandoned mine. Immediately stakes which formerly could have been bought for a few dollars brought $4000 a foot. A dozen penniless prospectors thus became rich men within a week.

As he lounged on the plaza Sam had often seen wagons piled high with bricks of silver. The ore came from Gold Hill, which had made many a miner wealthy. Suddenly attention turned elsewhere and the name *Humboldt* rang through the town. Humboldt Mountain, some two hundred miles northwest of Carson City, was said to have lodes so rich that every hundred pounds of ore contained silver worth two to three hundred dollars. This was the news which aroused Sam. A newly opened mine might have possibilities for a prospector.

Every hour of every day Sam's imagination throbbed to the excitement swirling through the plaza. Storekeepers, barbers, hostlers, barkeepers talked of giving up their occupations to go prospecting. One noon the boardinghouse table fairly rocked with discussion of the report in a newspaper brought to town that morning. When Sam was asked if he had read it, he replied by quoting the last paragraph: " 'Have no fear of the mineral resources of Humboldt County. They are immense, incalculable.' "

Sitting next to Sam was a young lawyer named Billy Clagget, a recent arrival whom he had known in Keokuk. In a low tone he said, "This report has convinced me. Only a fool would waste such a chance. I'm going to Humboldt and buy a ledge or stake a claim, or whatever you do. I really am."

It was the spark necessary to start Sam's resolution. "Suppose I go along. Let's start right away."

Clagget knew another lawyer, A. W. Oliver. He, too, had caught fire. As the three began to work out plans, they were joined by a stouthearted old fellow named Tillou, a blacksmith by trade. In a few days the four gamblers had acquired two horses and a cart, mining tools, pickaxes, and supplies of food. At the last moment Watts' book of hymns, a cribbage board, and a keg of beer were heaved into the wagon.

One December morning, amid the cheers of all the businessmen around the plaza, the party set forth with the jauntiest possible air. After a few miles the mood changed. There were no roads across the plain. The struggling old horses pulled the heavy cart so slowly through the sand that each man in turn had to help them by pushing it.

After the sand came steep uphill roads, and the nights grew painfully cold. One day a terrifying band of Indians surrounded the party, but fortunately they accepted gifts of flour and sugar in place of scalps. The only bright hour of each tiresome day came after supper around a campfire. Then everyone sang songs and Sam was in his glory as a spinner of tales.

Hardship did not dim the party's determination. Neither did the aspect of the mining village, which consisted of eleven cabins facing one another at the bottom of a deep gorge. The newcomers at once set to work building a similar cabin. They left a hole in the canvas roof and under the hole on the dirt floor they lighted a fire whenever they could find brushwood or buy it from the Indians. When the cabin was completed, prospecting started under the guidance of the more experienced Tillou.

Just one day of tramping over snow-covered rocks, pausing only to use pickax and shovel at the spots Tillou selected, filled Sam's whole being with bitter disappointment. Long afterward he confessed that he had supposed chunks of silver would provide visible evidence of the right place to open up a mine. Grimly and gamely he followed the guide in the exhausting, fruitless search which went on for days on end. Then at last Tillou found a promising ledge and the backbreaking work began. They tunneled into the rock with pickaxes until the crevice was deep enough so that dynamite powder could be used.

Facing the other three miners one evening as they sat around the fire, Tillou said, "Trouble is, the silver vein in this quartz rock is too deep for our tools. To reach it, we'd have to sink a shaft. That would cost us too much unless we got proof that a rich lot of silver is down there. I think the best way is to claim the ledge right now and see if we can't find some other claims that ain't so good, but might sell."

It was agreed. Notices of their discovery of the valuable ledge were put up and copies with their four names were sent to the mining recorder's office. The search for likely claims then went on and a number were put up for sale in Humboldt. No takers bought them, and the quartet were on the brink of starvation.

One night Sam said, "My brother and I once bought several feet in different locations of the Esmeralda mine. Maybe they might prove better than Humboldt. The assays show a rich strain in the Esmeralda lode."

"Assays!" Tillou snorted. "I'll tell you about them. A man brings in a few rocks to be assayed. He's picked 'em out of a couple of tons because they show a little gold. So he gets a fine report to brag about and makes some poor devil think every ton in the claim will be a jewel box. So he buys it. Yah! Assays!"

Sam sprang up and began pacing up and down the shack. "But that's just the kind of game we're trying to play. We've learned the real secret of success in silver mining. It isn't labor by the sweat of our hands, but the sale of ledges to poor toiling slaves who will do the real work."

Billy Clagget and his pal laughed lightheartedly at this

summary, but Sam glared at them. "I can't keep on with this gamble. I'm going back to Carson City and see what our Esmeralda claims are worth and maybe do some honest-to-goodness mining."

"I'll go, too," said Tillou. "I'll buy us horses with what we got left, you and me, Sam, and we'll go."

The two young attorneys chose to stay in the town of Humboldt and practice law. Friendly good-bys and best wishes were exchanged. Down the mountain went the riders and after a few miles they found themselves in a heavy snowstorm. It lasted three days, and each night both men believed that they and their horses would freeze to death before morning. They plowed on, however, and the storm ceased before they reached the valley. On the Carson River they found an inn and stopped there to rest themselves and the weary horses.

Hardly had they put their horses in the stable and set down their own packs when twenty wagons drove up. Soon a crowd of teamsters and two Overland stagecoach drivers stormed in for supper, followed by a number of nondescript tramps. They were all so brutally rough in talk and behavior that Sam was not only revolted, but also fearful of trouble to come.

As soon as he and Tillou had downed their rabbit stew and bread pudding, they strolled off to visit a nearby Indian camp they had heard about. The clear beauty of the sunset sky was a happy change from snowstorms. Following the Carson River, they noticed how low the water was in its narrow bed. Immediately a strange scene at the camp came into view. Squaws with papooses on their backs were rolling up blankets and packing up kits of food—all in a mad hurry. Men were loading all the tepees on makeshift sledges to which horses were hitched.

As politely as possible, with smiles and gestures, Sam asked a stalwart chieftain why the tribe was leaving in such a hurry. With a grunt the man pointed to the creek. "Heap big water come," he said.

Turning back toward the inn, Sam said to his companion, "What does he mean? Sounds crazy. A clear night, a creek almost dry. How could he be afraid of a flood?"

Back in their room, the weary travelers fell asleep instantly. At about midnight they were awakened by an uproar outside. Men were shouting, cows were mooing, and above all the other noises came the shrill neighing of horses. Tillou, who had dashed to the window, cried, "Look at the river!"

Bright moonlight illuminated a weird scene. Teamsters were fanning out in a huge semicircle to drive cattle and horses up the slope to the high ground on which the inn stood. Below, the Carson River had turned into a raging torrent bearing on its crest brush and forest rubbish. It was over its banks and beginning to lap the edge of the stable.

Sam and Tillou leaped down the stairs pell-mell and across the yard into water reaching their knees. Splashing into the stable, they led their own terrified horses up to the rear of the inn, tied them, and rushed back to help rescue the other horses. Above the shouts and the cries of animals rose a yell of welcome as a big fellow swam from one of the farm sheds to the slope's edge. As he reached safe land, the shed collapsed with a crash of timbers. He had been asleep in the shed and had not awakened until water inundated his straw mattress.

When nothing more could be done, the crowd gathered on the porch of the inn to gaze about in wonder. The place had become an island in a moonlit lake.

Stumbling wearily into bed at last, Sam remarked, "Tillou, how did those Indians know a flood was coming? If they hadn't, all of them would have been drowned."

"Maybe their gods warned 'em," muttered the old man.

For eight intolerable days no one could leave the inn. It was a prison jammed with men who drank, gambled, swore, and quarreled away the dreary hours. One man called Arkansas seemed so eager to use the two revolvers fastened to his belt and the bowie knife peeking from one boot top that the other teamsters, hardened as they were, grew uneasy. One afternoon he deliberately drove the landlord into an argument until one of his replies could be twisted into an insult. Then out came the ready pistol.

"Don't shoot, Arkansas," screamed the terrified victim. "I didn't mean nothin' wrong. Don't shoot!"

But Arkansas pulled the trigger. Luckily the shot hit only an empty bottle on the bar counter. The landlord jumped from behind the bar, over chairs and benches, and through

the shouting crowd. Arkansas fired at him again, but he was too drunk to aim accurately and the bullets were buried in the wooden wall. The landlord pulled open a door to the kitchen and banged it after him with a crash of shattered glass from the window in the door. Five seconds later Arkansas flung the door open.

On the threshold the landlord's wife confronted him, pointing a pair of sharp scissors at his breast. Arkansas halted in surprise, then stepped backward. The woman advanced upon him with the silent intentness of an animal trainer as the hushed crowd watched in amazement. Suddenly, while she backed him into the center of the room, her tight lips opened and she delivered a volley of scorn and abuse which seemed to stupefy the huge fellow. He stood bewitched until she turned on her heel and strode to the kitchen amid cheers from the onlookers. From then on Arkansas was a crushed and quiet man.

At last the flood receded and the long-suffering innkeeper was left in peace as everyone departed. Sam and the blacksmith were so glad to escape that they faced the perils of the return journey with undaunted spirits. Once they nearly drowned in a branch of the swollen Carson River. Time after time they thought their horses were at the end of their strength. Yet one day they finally galloped into the plaza of Carson City.

Within a fortnight Sam was off again to prospect on the Esmeralda. He started with a small party headed by Captain Nye, the Governor's brother. Nye settled in a camp some nine miles from the one which Sam shared with a very experienced prospector named Higbie. From the first both young men were pursued by misfortune. The footage once purchased by the Clemens brothers proved absolutely worthless. The few new claims Sam could afford to buy, in the hope of a quick sale, remained unwanted on his hands. His funds grew so low that he took a job as day laborer at a mill where silver and mercury were extracted from quartz rock. After a week he quit, exhausted.

Higbie fared no better. The two partners joined a group on a mad hunt for a mysterious cement mine said by all the other prospectors to contain rich veins of gold. But the mine was not located.

After their return to the Esmeralda, Higbie actually discovered a rich vein of silver. They registered their claim at once. In order to hold it they were obliged by law to start mining operations within ten days. Higbie went off in high spirits to buy tools on credit, leaving Sam to write triumphantly to Orion that at last they had struck it rich. Before he had finished the letter a man on horseback arrived at the cabin with an urgent message from Captain Nye. He had been taken seriously ill and had sent for young Clemens to come at once to help nurse him. Partly from his own friendly concern, partly because for Orion's sake he couldn't refuse to help the Governor's brother, Sam agreed to go.

"I don't think I'll be kept long, partner," he wrote to Higbie, "but I'll have to depend on you to start work on the mine. Don't put it off. This is our big chance."

Eight days passed before Nye was well enough so that Sam could leave him. It was evening on the ninth day when Sam entered the cabin he shared with his partner. Higbie was just lighting a lantern. "How much work did you get done on our claim?" he asked Sam.

"Didn't you get my note?" Sam exclaimed. "Haven't you been working? Where have you been?" They stared at one another in horror. Higbie had to confess that he had taken one more gamble—said to be a sure thing this time—on finding the cement mine. He had not seen Sam's note, but had left one of his own, urging Sam to save the claim by doing some mining work.

Cursing the luck, cursing his partner, Sam stamped around the shack in a fury of disappointment. "We've lost it!" he roared. "Tomorrow is the tenth day."

They had, indeed, lost their claim and they had not found the cement mine, either. Mournfully, the next day, they began to plan what they would do next. In the midst of the discussion, Sam remembered that he had received a letter from Joseph Goodman, editor of the *Territorial Enterprise*. This was a first-rate daily published in Virginia City, some hundred miles north of Carson City. He had read the letter carelessly during the excitement of registering the ill-fated claim. Now he got it out and gloomily considered it.

Ever since he returned from Humboldt, Sam had, on Orion's advice, sent short, amusing satires on Western characters to the *Enterprise*. He himself didn't think too highly of these rough sketches, but it was fun to see them in print. He signed them with the name Josh. His latest one was a burlesque of a rabble-rousing orator. Sam had him open his speech by roaring, "I was sired by the American Eagle and foaled by the Continental Dam." Evidently this had delighted the editor, for he had written to invite Mr. Samuel Clemens to join the staff of the newspaper as city editor at a salary of twenty-five dollars a week.

A fortnight ago, with a half share of a rich silver lode apparently assured, the offer had been put aside to wait until Sam found time to write a polite refusal. But now that he was without a penny and had no prospects in view, he knew he ought to think about the proposal. It meant security, at least.

Stuffing the letter in his pocket, Sam said to Higbie, "Well, I've spent half a year prospecting, with nothing gained and money lost. All the same, I hate to admit a failure. I still believe in the Esmeralda. But I need time to decide about things. I'm going off for a bit to think."

When he returned from a sojourn in the wilderness, Higbie said, "You sure look like you been wrastlin', boy!"

Sam grinned. "You know it isn't easy to give up a gamble like prospecting. But I've come to believe I'd never be any good at it. So I've decided to take the job on the *Enterprise*. Only the angels know if I'm wise."

Orion thought he was. Sam started off on his hundred-mile walk to Virginia City with his brother's affectionate blessing.

One hot August day Mr. Samuel L. Clemens entered the

handsome new building of the *Territorial Enterprise* and sank into a chair. He dropped his heavy pack, containing blankets, canteen, and clothing, on the floor beside him.

In obvious astonishment a young man sitting behind a desk looked up and asked, "What may I do for you, sir?"

Sam smiled faintly. Well he knew the impression he must be making. Unshaven and uncombed, dusty from head to foot, dressed in a rumpled blue shirt and greasy trousers tucked into shabby boots, he was the perfect image of a vagabond.

"I'd like to see Mr. Goodman," he said slowly. "My name is Clemens and I have been asked to join the editorial staff."

Only in the Far West, where anybody in any guise was apt to turn up, would he have been accepted without proving his identity. Instantly the young man sprang up, held out his hand, and said cordially, "Welcome! You're Josh of the comic letters, aren't you? I'm Steve Gillis. Mr. Goodman will soon be here and meanwhile I'll show you around our place."

One day later the hobo had been transformed into a man about town. His flowing ragged beard was reduced to a reddish mustache matching his well-clipped hair. In a gleaming white shirt, cutaway coat, dark, well-pressed trousers, and shining black shoes, he was the best-dressed member of the *Enterprise* staff.

During a serious interview with Joe Goodman on his first morning Sam learned that he was expected to be a reporter as well as editor of local news. The *Enterprise* had earned its notable success, he was told, by printing only the truth. Rumors were never accepted. Every news story had to be based on facts. Personal opinions were quoted only when individual names could be used. Firsthand investigation of all events was required. Of course, Goodman explained with a friendly smile, the flights of fancy which made the "Josh" letters popular were in a different category and that kind of humor was much desired.

Sam's first week on the job was spent in learning about Virginia City. He had never imagined such a place. It was built in tiers halfway up the side of a mountain, and underneath it lay the celebrated Comstock lode of silver and gold, named for its discoverer, a mad miner who never made a cent from it. Although it had been discovered only three years before, every mine within the mountain was being worked night and day, by shifts of highly paid laborers. Hundreds of feet below the houses and streets of the town blasting and shoveling went on without cease. Every day tons of ore were hauled to the surface by windlasses and carried down to the mills by mule teams.

The business section of the city, made up of stores, hotels, boardinghouses, saloons, and gambling parlors, had a reckless gaiety and color all its own. Everyone who lived there and every visitor passing through was a speculator in mining stock or in claims. If a prospector found a promising ledge he could immediately sell a few feet of it for a large price, without a single proof of its worth.

In his letters to Orion and to the family in St. Louis Sam described the flush times in Virginia City. Nobody was poor and silver dollars were tossed around like popcorn. There was always some excuse for a parade with brass bands blaring and a military company marching before the town officials. A large opera house offered almost nightly performances of dramas, operas, or what were called musical entertainments.

The new editor had not been long at work when a silver lode was discovered in the neighboring region. Settlers there called it Silver City. Naturally the fever of speculation in Virginia City became hotter than ever as soon as the discovery was reported. Sam visited all the mines from time to time. Holding to the standards set by the *Enterprise,* he never exaggerated the worth of a claim. But whenever he could honestly praise a well-dug tunnel or say that a ledge he had seen in Silver City seemed a little like the Comstock rock, he was sure to have an office visit from a grateful prospector. The two would exchange jokes, Sam would learn something new about mining operation, and when the visitor rose to depart he would insist upon Sam's accepting a certificate of footage in the mine. It was no use refusing. Indeed, refusal was considered almost an insult. Such gifts were the custom in this region of prosperity and were made with the casual air of offering a cigar. Sam sent most of his salary to his mother and Orion and lived on handouts from speculators.

Although he was amused by life in Virginia City, he was

always aware of its lunatic character. It was a dangerous place. In saloons and gambling dens a deadly fight was likely to start at any moment. Every man carried at least one revolver and quarrels frequently ended in death. What shocked Sam most was that in the eyes of many miners, merchants, and barkeepers, desperate characters had immense prestige. They were greeted and served like princes. "He got his man" was the phrase murmured admiringly as a bloodthirsty swashbuckler passed by. Trials for murder were burlesques of justice, for most of the assassins were judged guiltless.

The other men on the newspaper staff were friendly, congenial fellows, hard workers, intelligent, if not in the least cultured, and always ready for a good time. After the paper went to press the whole staff would gather to sing sad and merry songs and talk over the events of the day. To a man they delighted in the humorous skits, jokes, and hoaxes contrived by their new member. So did subscribers to the paper.

"But you must sign these contributions!" said Goodman. "Since you won't use Josh any longer, think up another pen name."

In a few days Sam announced it—Mark Twain. He explained that when the leadman on a Mississippi steamboat called out those words, they meant that there were twelve feet of water—safe going, at least at the moment. Editor, staff, and public approved. After seeing the name in several issues of the *Enterprise*, people identified it with Sam

Clemens, and gradually everyone began calling him Mark instead of Sam.

Goodman was persuaded to let him report the fall session of the legislature at Carson City and to sign his stories with the new pen name. Sam stayed with his brother, who was now well settled in a house with his wife Molly and his little daughter Jennie, who had finally joined him. It was pleasant to be with them and the legislative session was interesting.

At the first meeting someone clapped Sam on the back with a cordial greeting. He whirled about. "Bill Clagget!" he cried. "You old rascal, what's happened to you since Tillou and I left you. Are you a member of this legislature now?"

Bill, now a successful lawyer in Humboldt, had got himself elected to the legislature. He introduced Sam to the speaker of the assembly and both men kept Sam informed about the inner workings of territorial politics. This made it possible for "Mark Twain" to uncover many an attempt at graft and help defeat the passage of unfair bills. By the time young Clemens had reported a second legislative session, he had become something of a power for justice. Both his own fame and the increased influence of the *Enterprise* had spread far over the West.

When Sam said to Bill Clagget, "I'm not the numskull about mining that I was once," he referred to serious studies he had made of the mines in and near Virginia City. He was now familiar with the long process of digging and blasting out rock and extracting the precious ore to be molded into blocks. It was exciting to prowl around the network of excavations far down in the depths of the mountain. He liked and respected the skillful miners. They were a relief from speculators.

In spite of the utterly materialistic and irrational conditions of life which he so despised in Virginia City, Sam continually was exhilarated by the personal freedom that was possible there. It accounted for the individuality of men and women at every social level. His sharp observation and alert ear for variations of speech had plenty of practice. Whenever he returned to the office after an hour on the plaza he would say, "I've been watching a circus and theatrical performance combined." One of the acts was the coming and going of huge freight wagons drawn by twelve horses. Teamsters earned high pay, and the swagger with which they entered a saloon or a restaurant afforded the observer constant entertainment.

Most Americans in Nevada were not only self-centered, but strangely detached from the nation. California and Oregon had been admitted to the Union, but the rest of the enormous country of the West was awaiting exploration and settlement. These occupations were so absorbing that small attention was paid to events east of the Rocky Mountains. The mighty Civil War, which was to determine the nation's fate, was rarely discussed in Virginia City. The latest discovery of a silver lode or the latest murder, even the best joke, won more general attention than Lee's brilliant strategy and Grant's tightening grip on the Mississippi.

Undoubtedly Sam Clemens suffered from a sense of guilt because he took no part in the conflict. He seldom joined in discussions of the war held by fellow members of the newspaper's staff. They, at least, followed its progress as news came in over the telegraph wire. On the evening of July 4, however, he was startled and moved to see, on the very crest of the mountain towering over Virginia City, the Stars and Stripes aglow in the sunset light. Later he found out that the flag served as a silent celebration for the fall of Vicksburg and the triumph of Union forces in the great battle of Gettysburg.

During that year of 1863 Sam had begun to suffer from restlessness. A long visit from the famous humorist, Artemus Ward, who was riotously entertained by the *Enterprise* boys, increased Mark Twain's dissatisfaction with mere reporting. Ward kept urging him to use his talents more diversely. When he found out that Mark had had a few Western sketches published in a New York magazine, he insisted that his young friend should go ahead with his writing.

Gradually Mark became convinced that he must take a look at San Francisco and then return to the East. Suddenly fate gave him a violent push. Mark had ridiculed in print the editor of a rival newspaper, and the editor published an insulting retort. Soon, according to the gentlemanly custom of Nevada, pistols were substituted for words, and

Mark had issued two challenges to a duel. Steve Gillis cleverly managed to scare the editor into patching up the quarrel. As for the second challenge, Sam was warned that before the duel could take place, a law forbidding dueling, just passed by the legislature, would be enforced. He was almost commanded by his editor to leave town.

Steve Gillis went with him, "just on a jaunt." He wanted to see his brother, a miner, who lived in the hills of central California. Goodman, who hated to have his most popular writer depart, decided he would accompany Mark Twain, "just for the ride," in the Overland coach. It was a pleasant trip. Mark was never more lively. Possessed of health, funds, and a backlog of experience, he looked forward to exploring the future. It was late spring in the year 1864.

CHAPTER · · · · · · · SEVEN

San Francisco was a city radiant with flowers, a city climbing up steep hills to look down on the Golden Gate to the Pacific Ocean. Sam Clemens found its location and climate superb, its aspect picturesque. For many days he reveled in walking about the town and dining at the best restaurants. Newsmen who had read his articles in the *Enterprise* welcomed him cordially. They took him up to one of the city heights where wealthy people lived in mansions which were to become ever more elaborate with the passage of time. Although the owners had laid the foundations of their fortunes during the gold rush, they were based, not on mining speculations, but on the sale of merchandise to the forty-niners. Governor Leland Stanford, a man of

great presence, and Mark Hopkins were two of the most
distinguished millionaires.

Idleness soon palled on the pair from Virginia City. Sam
and Steve Gillis both went to work for the *Morning Call*,
a daily newspaper. Steve served as compositor and Sam as
reporter. They shared a room and had many good times
together. Steve's only complaint about his roommate was
that he read too much and too late.

For a while Sam liked the task of delving into the city's
vivid life. But he soon began to hate the required visits to
the police court every morning. The hours spent this way
passed in a sad monotony of accusations against drunks,
petty thieves, and other sordid sinners. It seemed to him
that police testimony was prejudiced and that the court
was apt to pass sentences too swiftly for justice. Chinese
and other foreign-born persons were never sure of a fair
trial.

He was pleased at first, however, by his evening assignment to review all the current plays, operas, and concerts.
Steve teased him unmercifully about it. "You a music
critic!" he laughed. "Why, all you know about music is
old songs like the one about the grasshopper and the ditty
about the horse 'named Methisodem, sold in Jerusalem.' "

Without denying his ignorance, Sam declared he was
impressed by the range of musical interest in this young
city of the Far West. Through his immediate friendship
with Thomas Maguire, an energetic theatrical producer,
he learned much about these cultural activities.

"I stick to presenting dramas," said Maguire, "and the Bianchi Company takes care of music—though they often rent my building. Funny, isn't it, that folks here are so set on opera? Why, even ten years ago, when the gold rush was bringing us the rabble, Verdi's opera, *Ernani*, was sung to big crowds and from then on operas drew full houses."

"Yes," agreed Sam, "I've had to go every night to this thing they're putting on now—*Belisario* by Donizetti, if that's the way you pronounce 'em—and the house was packed each time."

San Francisco also boasted a gifted conductor who had organized an excellent orchestra, gave frequent concerts, and had trained a chorus to sing Haydn's oratorio, *The Creation*.

It was a relief to Sam when a touring troupe of opera singers turned up. He was tortured by the necessity of attending the same performance every night and then devising some new comment about it. "I'm just a machine," he would moan to Steve, when they met for a midnight snack. "The editor pushes a button and out must come my story. I can't stand this job."

Nevertheless, he had to stand it for some time. Once again riches had escaped him. He held on too long to his gilt-edged shares in the largest Comstock mining company. Their fictitious value suddenly slumped and Sam's fictitious fortune was wiped out.

Moreover, just then Orion chose to renounce the only chance the Clemenses had ever had to profit by possession of the Tennessee lands. He firmly refused a good offer for the tract. The prospective buyer wished to grow grapes on the 3000 acres—grapes for wine. Orion, an impassioned prohibitionist, scorned financial advantage based on what he considered wickedness. The fact that he deprived the family of needed funds was of no importance to him. Sam's fury was violent and his present existence seemed more than ever a dreary desert waste.

There was, however, one gleam of sunshine. Sam had been quickly drawn into a literary group whose distinction was unrivaled in the country west of New England. Many of its numbers, topped by Bret Harte and Ambrose Bierce, were destined to reach national fame. For a time two magazines, the *Golden Era* and the *Californian*, backed by men of means, published contributions from these talented young men. Charles Henry Webb, publisher of the *Californian*, became Sam's special friend and an admirer of his amusing sketches. Such fellowship offered nourishment to his creative gift.

For a fortnight even straight reporting suddenly became exciting. One morning as Sam was walking down Telegraph Hill the pavement suddenly heaved up under his feet. Weaving about like a drunken man, he saw, with startled eyes, the entire front of a building some yards away fall forward in a solid block, covering the street with bricks. Before he could right himself on the convulsed sidewalk, men, women, and children had begun running into the street. Some of them had obviously just jumped out of bed. "An earthquake!" cried Sam. He was taut with excitement over such a dramatic new experience.

From that moment on he went about for days to report damage and collect odd and often funny tales from inhabitants. Fortunately, the earthquake had spent most of its energy in freakish pranks. Few houses and business buildings were destroyed and few people injured. With characteristic Western energy hundreds of men began at once to make repairs.

After that thrilling episode routine work for the *Morning Call* became more boring than ever. Sam began to neglect assignments and presently, with the agreement of the editor, his engagement ceased. As soon as Joe Goodman heard that Sam was free, he offered to take him back on the *Enterprise* as daily correspondent from San Francisco. Sam was assured absolute freedom as to what he chose to write.

Rushing to tell his literary friends of this interesting assignment, he cried, "Here's my chance to unveil the devil and his works."

With the holy joy of a crusader Sam began a series of relentless attacks on the corruption of the San Francisco government. The facts and their consequences were set down with a pen dipped in vitriol. His revelations were discussed throughout the entire West. All the officials of San Francisco were furious, and Martin G. Burke, the chief of police, started a libel suit against the *Territorial Enterprise*. This delighted Joe Goodman, who wrote to his correspondent that the suit was benefiting the paper by bringing it immense publicity and excellent sales.

A typically Western incident halted the sensational series. Steve got into a violent row with a barkeeper who was an ardent vote getter for the police chief. Burke had Steve Gillis arrested on grounds of assault with intent to kill, and of course Sam Clemens went bail for his friend. Then a man Steve knew in the city government warned him that he hadn't a chance in the world for a fair trial, and Steve slipped out of town, bound for Virginia City. Immediately Burke took legal action to collect the bail from Sam Clemens. This meant ruin. Sam was advised by friends and acquaintances to leave San Francisco until the trouble blew over. Steve's brother, Jim Gillis, a miner who had come to San Francisco to help Steve, was delighted to carry Sam off to his cabin in the Tuolumne hills.

To a man used to rough living, the sojourn with Jim Gillis offered idyllic peace. Jim and his partner were permanently engaged in an enterprise called pocket mining. It was often pursued in regions where there were abandoned mines. All it consisted of was shoveling up dirt that looked promising to the practiced eye, dumping it into a huge sieve, flushing it with water, and then picking out any gold nuggets too big to fall through the wire. This treasure hunt produced just enough reward to satisfy the partners' trifling needs. The simplest food and cheapest tobacco contented them. They worked and loafed in carefree rhythm and their guest gratefully slipped into the restful life.

Now and then Sam went out prospecting with them and carried pails of water to flush the sieve. Gradually he became infected by the quiet charm of pocket mining. For weeks he tramped with his friends on an ambitious prospecting tour near Angel's Camp, in central California's mountainous region. All the forest scenery was beautiful and Sam was awe-struck by the stupendous trees and thrilling waterfall in the valley which is now Yosemite National Park.

That was where this vagabond, as he called himself, was wandering while the most dramatic events in his nation's history were taking place. Neither telegraph nor postal service reached him with the news that on Palm Sunday, April 9, 1865, Robert E. Lee surrendered his army to General Grant. Weeks passed before Sam learned that on Good Friday, April 14, President Lincoln was assassinated. He could not follow in imagination the funeral train as it moved slowly westward from Washington to be met at every way station by crowds gathered in silence and tears. Indeed, before he even returned to the camp, a program of vengeance against the South had begun at the national capital and Lincoln's plea for "malice toward none" and "charity for all" was violently denied.

Slowly Sam became convinced of the utter futility of pocket mining and declared that he must get back to San Francisco. His last day of treasure hunting was spent on a pocket which Gillis was certain would prove to be rich. For hours Sam struggled up steep slopes with pails of water for flushing the sieve. Finally, cold and exhausted, he set down the pails with unusual firmness. "This is the last, Jim," he declared. "I'm through."

"Oh, just one more!" begged the others. But Sam was obdurate. Sorrowfully Jim posted the claim, with three names signed to it, and left the half-filled sieve where it was on the mountainside.

Of course the miners intended to return as soon as they had seen Sam on his way. When they finally did so it was to learn that two wandering prospectors had found in the sieve, now washed by rain, a goodly number of gold nug-

gets. After the legal thirty days had passed, they made off
with the treasure. When Sam heard of the loss, he knew
with absolute certainty that he was fated to miss every
possibility of gain from any sort of mining operation.

At San Francisco he found certain changes for the better
among the city officials. The old political factions, however, were still in power. When Goodman engaged Sam
again as a correspondent, he still found plenty to criticize,
but this time no protests were made. There was a letter from
Artemus Ward waiting for him. Ward had been preparing
for publication a collection of short pieces typical of American humor and had asked Mark Twain to send him a
story as soon as possible.

"Of course it's too late now to make the publication
date," Mark said to Bret Harte, "but I'm going to write
a story for him anyhow. It was told me by an old fellow at
a tavern near Angel's Camp."

The story, known as "The Jumping Frog," could not
be included in Ward's book, which had already gone to
press, but it was published in a New York newspaper.
Immediately, to the author's amazement, the "Frog" was
so praised, copied, and laughed over that Mark Twain's
name began to be known in the East. Its success had the
effect of increasing his longing for a new field of journal-
ism. After six months in San Francisco he determined to
launch out and he had a definite plan for so doing.

He went to Sacramento to consult the editors of the

Union, an excellent daily paper. They had long been his admiring friends and they were easily persuaded to accept his proposal. Maintaining that interest in the Sandwich Islands, now called the Hawaiian Islands, should be stimulated with a view to linking them some day to the United States, Sam believed he could send from Honolulu a series of articles which would be popular with subscribers. With a contract in his pocket and good wishes from the editors echoing in his ears, he returned to San Francisco. On March 17 he sailed on a smart new steamer, the *Ajax,* and, halfway across the Pacific, landed on Oahu. He thought he had never seen anything more beautiful than Pearl Harbor.

From the moment Sam set foot on land the tranquil charm of Honolulu possessed him. His letters of introduction to the American minister and to other officials and his unexpected meeting of a few old friends provided him with plenty of social life. He said to one of his hosts, "Nobody here tears around trying to make money. What a blessed contrast to Carson City and San Francisco!"

His own work was pure pleasure. Just by strolling about he could find colorful material for an article. The market was bright with the gay costumes worn by native Hawaiians and by Chinese and Japanese. A formal call upon the King of Oahu provided another sketch. Elected to royal office by his people, the King was a charming, well-educated young gentleman, praised by all for the intelligence of his gentle rule.

From Honolulu he sailed to other islands. Hawaii, the largest of the group, offered the most varied points of interest. They ranged from a 16,000-foot snow-covered mountain to the spot where Captain Cook, the famous British navigator, was murdered by natives in 1778. Although Sam admired the forests, orange groves, and sugar plantations, surf bathing and ancient temples, his supreme experience was exploring the smoldering volcano of Kilauea. He joined an acquaintance in a daring night descent into the crater and a close approach to its lake of boiling lava. To look upward at the gorgeous bursts of flame, at fiery fountains veiled in pale-green and golden vapors gave him the mixed sensation of gazing at both hell and fairyland.

On the island of Maui he was one of a party which climbed ten thousand feet to the summit of a dead volcano. Waking at dawn, he was held in a spell of wonder at the effects of changing light. As the sun rose over the vast expanse of land and sea he felt with awe that he had seen the miracle of divine creation.

Walking and riding endless miles over rough mountain roads finally exhausted Sam's strength. He returned to Honolulu very ill. As he sank into bed at his hotel he murmured to the friend who had met him at the wharf, "I'm going to stay right here for a week."

The next morning he received a message from the American minister. The previous night two distinguished passengers had landed, Anson Burlingame, American ambassador to China, and General von Valkenburg, American ambassador to Japan. The message said that these gentlemen, having learned that Mark Twain was in Honolulu, wanted above all to meet him, because they admired his work. Therefore they wished to visit him at his hotel, since he was too ill to move.

But Sam did move. He struggled out of bed, bathed, shaved, dressed in his best suit, and had himself driven to the American embassy. To the shocked reproaches of the company he said, "Gentlemen, I couldn't let you do me so much honor."

Some time after the gay and delightful luncheon ended, there came news from the island of Hawaii which excited all Honolulu. A small open boat had landed there, bringing fifteen half-dead men. They had escaped from their burning vessel in early May with ten days' rations. The captain, first mate, two passengers, and eleven seamen, packed into the ship's longboat, had managed to sail it, and survive fearful seas, scorching sun, thirst, and near starvation for forty-three days on a four-thousand-mile voyage to find land.

"What a story!" Mark gasped. "The whole world ought to know it!"

Anson Burlingame nodded. Mark wanted to write that story. The ambassador thought there must be a way to help him get it, but Sam was too ill to travel to Hawaii. Next day he was decidedly worse and lay raging over the lost opportunity. Two days later eleven of the survivors were brought to the hospital in Honolulu and the ambassador to China hurried over to Mark. "Now," he told him, "you are going to get from these men the whole history of their survival. I have it all arranged."

Burlingame had a stretcher carry Mark to the hospital. Then he himself questioned one man after another while Mark, propped up on pillows, took notes. Hour after hour the interviews went on, until the disaster and the fearful voyage in the overloaded boat were pictured in every detail.

As Sam was carried out of the hospital, he said to his friend, "Mr. Burlingame, it was wonderful of you to do this. It's a marvelous tale. Of course, all the newspapermen here will try to get it. But I have it, and I'm going to write it in time to ship it on the *Ajax* tomorrow morning."

It was no idle boast. All through the night he wrote furiously. By morning he had two manuscripts copied and ready, one for the *Union* of Sacramento and the other for his old Nevada paper, the *Enterprise*. The thick envelopes were literally thrown on the *Ajax* as it slowly moved away from the wharf.

Mark Twain's vivid account of tragedy and triumph on the sea was a sensational newspaper scoop. It was telegraphed to most of the important papers in the United States, and the correspondent's name echoed in editorial offices and was remembered by thousands of readers.

"Now, sir," he said to the ambassador, "I guess I'd better float back on the crest of this wave before it subsides." He had recovered so rapidly from his illness that at a Fourth-of-July ball he danced all night.

A fortnight later he took passage to San Francisco on a

slow sailing boat. He had decided to write for *Harper's Magazine* an article based on the newspaper account and was glad of the time on shipboard to finish it. Fortunately one of the survivors who had been a passenger on the long-boat was also on the ship. He had kept a diary and he allowed Mark to use it. Excerpts from it added powerfully to the emotional effect of the story.

In a mood of elation Mark reached San Francisco. But from the little pinnacle on which he had perched, he immediately fell flat. It was strange to be without a newspaper connection. Yet he had no wish to return to any of his former jobs. He was convinced that the Western chapter of his writing life was finished. If only he could have saved enough money to go East at once! *Harper's Magazine* had accepted his sea story, but the check he received was pitifully small. How could he make some money? After days of gloom, he seized on a possible idea. Without much confidence in it, he went to consult his friend John McComb, publisher of the newspaper, *Alta California*.

"What would you think, John," he said hesitatingly, "of my trying a lecture on the Sandwich Islands?"

"Splendid!" cried the publisher. "Hire a big hall. Charge a dollar a ticket! It will be a huge success."

In utter amazement Sam stared at his friend. "Good glory!" he murmured. "You really mean it, don't you? Now I guess I'll have to go ahead."

His next move was to interview Tom Maguire, the producer. Shyly he presented his plan. "Great idea!" responded

Maguire. "We'll use the new opera house and fill it to the brim. Tell you what I'll do, Sam. I'll rent it to you at half price and still make money. It's a go!"

Speechless with surprise and gratitude, Sam hurried back to his hotel to write the lecture. The next day Maguire called him down to his office to work out the advertisements for the lecture on the Sandwich Islands. Between them, in high spirits they wrote some big headlines followed by lines in fine print:

A SPLENDID ORCHESTRA
is in town, but has not been engaged.

ALSO
A DEN OF FEROCIOUS WILD BEASTS
will be on exhibition in the next block.

MAGNIFICENT FIREWORKS
were in contemplation for this occasion
but the idea has been abandoned.

A GRAND TORCHLIGHT PROCESSION
may be expected; in fact, the public are
privileged to expect whatever they please.

Dress Circle $1.00.   Family Circle $.50.

Doors open at 7 o'clock.   The trouble begins at 8 o'clock.

On the evening announced, long before the opera-house doors opened, Mr. Mark Twain was hiding off stage in a trembling, terror-stricken condition. At five minutes to eight o'clock he forced himself to peek from behind the wings. What he saw was not the empty house he expected, but a house packed to the doors. Gathering up all his store of courage, he proceeded on wobbly legs to the front of the stage. A storm of applause rocked him for a moment. Then he realized he was among friends and relaxed. The lecture, which combined eloquent descriptions of scenery and native customs with amusing incidents told with wittily turned phrases, delighted the audience. It was interrupted constantly by roars of laughter and rounds of applause. The next day all the San Francisco papers praised the lecture so warmly that Sam began to wonder if a brief career of lecturing might bring in some real money.

He was not alone in this idea. A friend who had once been on the *Territorial Enterprise* hurried to see him. "Mark Twain, your lecture was absolutely great. You must go on a tour of the West. Let me manage it and we'll make plenty."

No further persuasion was necessary. For weeks the two men traveled to towns near San Francisco and to a few mining camps. Everywhere entire communities turned out and enthusiasm waxed. Each time Mark spoke, he was drier, funnier, and more eloquent. On they went to Nevada, where he was welcomed as a favorite son. In Virginia City and Carson City the opera houses were jammed. In every possible way it was a rewarding tour. Sam returned to San Francisco with a single driving purpose—to go home. He set off on December 17.

He had chosen to return by the water route. After the long voyage down to Nicaragua, passengers were transferred to a small vessel which crossed Lake Nicaragua and then went down the San Juan River. Another ship took the passengers to a place near the coast. There lines of carriages waited to convey passengers and luggage to the harbor where the ship for New York was anchored. In a rainstorm the passengers were loaded into surf boats to be taken out to the steamer. For forty-eight more years, until the Panama Canal was opened for traffic, travelers made this tedious crossing between the Pacific and the Atlantic Oceans.

Before many days had passed it was learned that cholera had broken out among the poor wretches in the steerage. In no time the ship's hospital was full and soon medicines gave out. On the eleven-day trip twenty-six victims died. A number of them were travelers in the first class.

When the ill-fated steamer landed at Key West, many terrified passengers left it. Although Sam was one of those who had the courage to stay on board, he had never felt greater relief than when he walked down the gangplank to a wharf jutting into New York's Hudson River. "Twenty-eight days out of San Francisco!" he exclaimed to a fellow passenger. "A trip to Europe will be a ferry ride in comparison."

Mark's first errand in New York was to see Charles Henry Webb, the man who had founded the *Californian*, a San Francisco magazine. Webb had been preparing for publication a number of Mark Twain's sketches, including "The Jumping Frog." After their conference Mark himself took the manuscript to Artemus Ward's publisher, but failed to place it. "All right," said Webb, "I'll bring it out myself."

Sam laughed, thanked him, and wished him luck. He didn't care too much about the little collection, for another project had been taking hold of his imagination. This was nothing less than a trip around the world. He believed it would offer material for a first-rate book. Even before he left San Francisco he had won a vague promise from the editor of *Alta California* to engage him as correspondent in case he made the journey. But he did nothing about the matter in New York; he was in a rush to get home. His impatience mounted hourly as the train snorted its way to St. Louis.

"Six years is a long time, Sam," said his mother as his arms went around her. "But you've been a good son about writing."

Sam turned smiling eyes upon his nephew. "Who is this young man? Not my namesake, Sam Moffett! How could he grow so tall behind my back?"

For days they exchanged news and jokes. Pamela laughed at her brother's yarns until tears rolled down her cheeks. Her solidly prosperous husband joined the general lament because Sam was going up to Hannibal. His friends there had arranged a lecture date for him, and after a pleasant visit with them he also lectured at Keokuk. Sam had begun to enjoy giving these talks. He was aware that there was a marked strain of the actor in him, and it amused him to use this talent to enhance his performance.

On his return to St. Louis he told the family about his plan to go around the world. Just as he had persuaded them that it was a most promising project, he gave it up for another one. One day when he was reading a St. Louis newspaper he sprang to his feet and ran into the hall. "Ma!" he shouted. "Here's something new, something great! You and Pamela come down and hear about it."

The article he had just read described an excursion to the Holy Land just being organized. The good ship *Quaker City*, with a "refined party," was to steam through the Mediterranean, with side trips to Paris, Rome, and Venice, and stops at Naples, Palermo, and northern Egypt. Then it would go on to Greece and the Holy Land. This was the very first excursion boat to Europe and the Middle East. The announcement made the trip sound like a superb holiday for the passengers.

"Isn't this wonderful?" cried Sam excitedly. "It's far better than a voyage around the world taken by oneself. I'm writing this very day to John McComb of the *Alta*, to get him to give me an assignment as a correspondent."

Jane Clemens listened to her son in astonishment. "But you'd use up all your pay in the fare. It sounds mighty expensive."

"Indeed I shan't!" he answered. "The *Alta* will have to

pay my fare and my salary, too. If they agree, I'll rush to New York."

"But why rush?" wailed Pamela. "The *Quaker City*, the paper says, isn't to sail till June."

He replied that if he was going to sail on it he would have a great deal to do in New York. But little did he know how much.

CHAPTER · · · · · · EIGHT

"Well, well, if it isn't Mark Twain himself! This is the jolliest thing that's happened since I left Salt Lake City!" With great thumps on the back, Frank Fuller, an old acquaintance, welcomed Sam to his New York office.

Six years before, when Fuller had been acting governor of Utah, the Clemens brothers had met him on their way out to Nevada. Later, Fuller's interest in the Comstock lode often took him to Virginia City. Many were the gay evenings he had spent with members of the *Territorial Enterprise* staff.

"I've been keeping track of you, Sam, ever since I came back East," he went on. "What are you doing here? You've had quite a career since I last saw you."

Sam told him about what had just happened. Colonel McComb, of the *Alta California,* had agreed to send him, passage paid, on the *Quaker City* tour. Each letter sent from abroad would earn twenty dollars and so would articles written in New York before sailing. At the New York bureau of the *Alta* he was given a check for $1200 to cover his round-trip ticket. Immediately he and the office chief went to arrange matters at the shipping office.

On the way, Sam declared that he might not qualify for membership in the excursion party. "You remember," he said with a quizzical grin, "that the *Quaker City* advertisement announced it would accommodate only 'refined persons.'"

In the shipping office the clerk was giving an interview to a newspaper reporter. He boasted about all the famous people booked for the excursion and wound up by saying, "And Mark Twain is going too."

After a visit to Charles Henry Webb, the publisher of his book, Sam met Fuller and told him the news. Fuller listened, then leaned forward and spoke earnestly. "Sam, you'll be in New York for weeks now. So you must give a lecture here on the Sandwich Islands. I've heard all about your successful tours in the West and I want to back you. I'll engage the Cooper Union Institute auditorium. It's the largest one in the city."

Mark blinked at him in astonishment. He was too frightened to even pretend that he was flattered by the proposal. When he found his voice he said, "No! Not on your life!"

He pointed out that he was utterly unknown in the East, it would be difficult to induce even a small audience to hear him, and absolutely impossible for him to fill a large hall.

Fuller swept his protests aside. "Nonsense! Your book will soon be out, and hundreds of people already know your 'Jumping Frog.' You'll draw a large crowd, I'm dead sure. Let's set a date right now. It ought to be in early May."

Little by little Sam felt himself dragged to the edge of the abyss. Fuller went ahead with plans and paid no heed to objections and warnings. Sam found himself committed to speak on a date three weeks hence, and he crept miserably out of the office. On the way back to his hotel, he went to Cooper Union and glanced at the auditorium. To imagine himself on the rostrum was misery. His letters to the family echoed his despair.

Soon Fuller began advertising Mark Twain's lecture for May 6. He lassoed every Californian in the city and made each one promise to attend it. He sent notices to newspapers and placed a bunch of handbills in horsecars and stages. Sam forced his manager to confess that expenses, including rental of the hall, had already approached five hundred dollars and that few tickets had been sold. Sam told him that of course they wouldn't sell, because on the same night New York theaters were offering such attractions as "The Black Crook," "The Fighting Scud," and a performance by some Japanese jugglers. How, Sam asked, could an unknown man expect patronage for a lecture on the Sandwich Islands? But Fuller only laughed and patted his shoulder.

On May first Charles Webb, the publisher, invited Sam to dinner and placed in his hand a little book bound in a blue and gold cover. "There you are, Mark," said Webb proudly. "How does it feel to be an author?"

Mark turned the book over in his slim, sensitive hands and fixed his eyes on the title, *The Celebrated Jumping Frog of Calaveras County and Other Sketches*. He looked up and smiled. "Thanks, Charles. It's a very pretty book. I might even read it sometime." Catching the disappointment in his friend's face, he leaned across the table to pat his arm. "Forgive me for not dancing a jig over this, Webb. I'll be doing that in six days. Now all I can think about is that horrible lecture."

Two days later he rushed into Fuller's office. "Frank," he shouted, "only a handful of tickets are sold. If I were brave enough to commit suicide I'd do it. You and I will be almost the only people in that gigantic auditorium. Something's got to be done. For the love of heaven *give* away tickets! Paper the house, man! Fill it somehow, or I'll run off to the woods."

Fuller nodded calmly. "Guess you've got a good idea there, boy. We really must have an audience. It isn't money that's so important on this occasion. It's a build-up of your prestige. I'm assuming all the expenses, so don't worry about that. But I will paper the house. Tell you what—I'll get you the most cultured audience imaginable. Today I'll send free tickets to all the schoolteachers in the city. And believe me, they'll be there."

Nevertheless, Sam spent the next two days pacing the floor of his room. On the scheduled night he and Fuller walked together in silence to Cooper Union. As they turned the last corner, Sam shrieked, "Look! Look at the carriages and cabs and the crowds! I can't believe it!"

A few moments later he stepped out on the platform to face some two thousand patrons and was deluged by a wave of cheers from the Californians. Doubts and fears

were swept away. Thrilled with excitement Mark Twain flung himself into his talk and for more than an hour held the huge audience breathless with interest and often convulsed with laughter. He could not remember enjoying an hour more.

Pushing through the clutter of admirers about the speaker, Frank Fuller caught him in a bear hug. "Great! Simply great!" he cried. Then, bending to whisper, he reported the good news that, after all, three fifths of the expenses had been covered by the purchase of tickets. Next day there was further cause for rejoicing. The most important newspapers printed full-length columns on the lecture and gave it hearty praise.

On the strength of this surprising success, Mark was able to make an arrangement for the *New York Tribune* to buy a number of articles from him on the trip to the Holy Land.

It was while he was at the *Tribune* building that he first met an attractive young journalist destined for a noted career as editor, author, and American ambassador. He was Whitelaw Reid.

Sam spent his next weeks in New York in frantic efforts to fulfill the *Alta* assignment for letters from New York. Refusing most invitations, he wrote night and day to complete eighteen articles and post them to California. The moment he had finished the task and made preparations for the voyage he fell prey to the same mood of inner bankruptcy which had often seized him in the mining districts and in San Francisco. He asked himself how he could have been so elated over the lecture at Cooper Union. What had he gained by signing up for a lot of newspaper pieces? Had he really ever done anything worth while?

His farewell letter to the family was a confession of all his faults, an outcry of remorse.

"If I could only say I had done one thing for any of you that entitled me to your good opinions (I say nothing of your love, for I am sure of that, no matter how unworthy of it I may make myself—from Orion down, you have always given me that all the days of my life, when God Almighty knows I have seldom deserved it) I believe I could go home and stay there. . . . You observe that under a cheerful exterior I have got a spirit that is angry with me and gives me freely its contempt."

Here was a revelation of the mysterious soul of Sam Clemens. His vision of man's possibilities for devotion to a great purpose was so clear that he could see egoistic satisfactions and failures in loving for what they are—sins against the spirit. At some level of consciousness he recognized his own materialistic ambition as pure illusion, and whenever he acted as if it were wise and right, guilt overtook him. On the other hand, his temperament enabled him to prize every new experience and to enjoy life as he found it.

No one meeting him on Saturday, June 8, in the lounge

of the *Quaker City* could possibly have suspected such undercurrents in this lively young man. He seemed immensely interested in both ship and passengers. Although a violent storm held the vessel in the harbor all the next day and night, Sam's mood was only slightly clouded. On Monday as the sailors weighed anchor and the ship began to move, as sunlight sparkled on the white-crowned waves, he felt such a rush of happiness that only consideration of others restrained him from bursting into song.

Every day he kept notes. In them a large proportion of the passengers were classified as pompous, boring, or ludicrously odd. There were fewer young people than old. Those who were neither proved to be the easiest to talk to. Mark at once made friends with the wife of a Middle Western newspaper publisher. With great interest in his assignments, she made an offer, which he gleefully accepted, to correct his letters before he mailed them. A man of his own age, from New York City, became Sam's chief pal. A youth named Charles Langdon, from Elmira, New York, began to follow Sam about to listen avidly to his droll remarks.

Week after week, after having crossed the Atlantic, the excursionists landed, went sight-seeing, and boarded the ship again to head for the next stop. Sam not only went everywhere and saw everything; before reaching an important place he assembled his knowledge of history and carefully studied guidebooks. Against the historical background he always estimated pictures, architecture, and the social scene. He tried to be fair. In spite of contempt for the institution of royalty, he freely admired the handsome improvements in Paris accomplished by Napoleon III. The poverty in Italy, however, afflicted him. He raged at the contrast between the pitiful beggars cluttering the steps of almost any great cathedral and the princely magnificence of the cathedral's interior. Resentfully he gazed at marble columns, superbly ornamented tombs, jeweled altars, delicate carvings, and gorgeous draperies.

On a visit to St. Peter's, he turned to Charley Langdon, who had accompanied him, to say in an angry undertone, "Why doesn't the church sell some of this jasper and lapis lazuli and oriental agate, and feed the hungry wretches we're always seeing? Why has Italy for centuries spent untold gold on churches and town halls and done nothing for its people but screw taxes out of them?"

Young Langdon murmured a protest about the glories of Renaissance art and the money and dignity given artists by their patrons. This defense elicited a snort from his companion. "Yes, a patron could make a great painter put those bloodcurdling Medici women right up in the clouds beside the Virgin Mary. Is that moral, let alone religious?"

Langdon wondered if the humorist had suddenly turned reformer. But once out in the sunshine again, Mark was as ready as ever to tease the party's guide with impossible questions which puzzled the poor fellow and drew roars of laughter from the excursionists. Charley was relieved at his companion's swift return to normal and, without understanding it, found this duality of temperament interesting.

One night when the *Quaker City* was anchored in the bay of Smyrna on the way to Constantinople (now Istanbul), the boy invited Mark to his stateroom. "I want to show you the things I picked up for the family," he said.

Sam was polite about the extravagant purchases. Suddenly he caught sight of a miniature perched on a shelf above the bunk. "May I look at this portrait?" he asked. "What a beautiful girl!"

"It's my sister Olivia," replied Charley. "She's a princess—and a saint, too. Unluckily, she isn't a bit strong. She's been sick a lot."

Sam stared long at the miniature and put it down reluctantly. "I've never seen a girl like that—so delicate, so, so non-earthy. I'll come and worship her again, if I may."

Many were the scenes during this expedition which stirred Sam deeply. A prowl around the ruins of Pompeii meant for him living through the last moments of terror and despair as Vesuvius rained hot lava upon the doomed citizens. On quite another plane of feeling was his impression of the Parthenon, seen first on a moonlight night. Standing on the crest of the celebrated hill, surrounded by the ghostly glories of that matchless civilization, he understood the deathless influence of Greece.

Of his view as he looked down at Athens in the mellow light, he wrote: "Overhead the stately columns, majestic still in their ruin . . . underfoot the dreaming city . . .

in the distance the silver sea. Not on the broad earth is there another picture so beautiful."

At last the excursion reached the Holy Land. For weeks beforehand Mark had been engaged in an intensive study of the Bible. At every halt he could relate the event which made it celebrated and even quote a Biblical passage. To ride slowly along the Sea of Galilee, to bathe in the Dead Sea, wade over the River Jordan, and cross the treeless plain where Christ and His disciples had traveled gave Sam the awed feeling of living again in that time.

Yet reverence was deflected all too often by some incident or by the absurd behavior of certain members of the party—especially as they scrambled aboard restive donkeys. The dreadful conditions of Arab villages horrified Sam and the insistent guides provoked him to comic sallies. Never were his shifts of mood so nerve-racking as at Jerusalem.

The party was led at once to the Church of the Holy Sepulcher. Practically every one of them was shocked to realize that its vast roof was supposed to shelter, not only the grave of Adam, but every hallowed spot involved in the last days of Christ's life on earth. Circling through the enormous edifice, the visitors were shown the prison where the Lord was scourged and mocked. They were then asked to gaze upon the True Cross and the very places where the risen Christ was met first by Mary Magdalene and then by His mother. At the center of the church stood the sepulcher of the crucified Christ.

Brooding sardonically on the incredible assemblage,

Sam walked about in lonely silence. He was outraged by the liberties churchmen had taken with those truths of history and geography set forth in the Scriptures, on maps, and in commentaries. Nonetheless, he was stirred to his marrow by the impact of the exhibition. His article about that visit was a bold satire on the impossible claim of authenticity for the display in the Church of the Holy Sepulcher.

Yet he ended his story by this comment: "[Here] . . . is the most sacred locality on earth to millions and millions of men and women and children, the noble and humble, bond and free. It is the most illustrious edifice in Christendom . . . because of the . . . veneration in which men hold the last resting place of the meek and lowly, the mild and gentle Prince of Peace."

Turning westward at last, the *Quaker City* anchored outside Alexandria long enough for passengers to visit the Pyramids and the Sphinx. In his account of this expedition Sam made the most of his combined talents.

His first compliments went to the common steed of Egypt: "I believe I would rather ride a donkey than any beast in the world. He goes briskly, he puts on no airs, he is docile, though opinionated. Satan himself could not scare him, and he is convenient—very convenient. When you are tired of riding you can rest your feet on the ground and let him gallop from under you."

He wrote a sidesplitting tale of climbing the Pyramid Cheops, but his portrait of the Sphinx was fine prose poetry.

That was the opinion of his mentor, the publisher's wife from Cleveland. She also commended his plan to write a book on the basis of his articles, which he told her confidentially.

"It's high time," he said, "for a realistic travel book to appear. We've all been brought up to expect Jerusalem to be a huge and mighty place—and how small and full of religious conflict it really is! As for what some so-called authorities on the Holy Land perpetrate. . . . Well! One of them has planted trees all over the deserts we crossed and pictured the gray, dull Sea of Galilee as a beautiful dark-blue lake. He's turned those ugly Arabian girls into stage beauties and lifted little Mount Hermon to Alpine heights. Such fact twisting is mighty hard on travelers. I mean to tell the public what is what. But of course, the book ought to have fun in it, too."

Mark knew the prospective book would have to be written in his spare time, for he had just accepted a job, by mail. He was to be secretary to Senator William Stewart, an old friend from Virginia City, who had been elected after Nevada became a state. Sam felt that he must have a job, and one that allowed him time to write. The day after the ship docked at New York, on November 19, he took a train to Washington.

At first he shared a room with Senator "Bill," who seemed only too glad to have his secretary make friends with newspapermen. Probably he never knew the bitter contempt Sam shared with them for the greedy, venal spirit of Congress during this last year of Andrew Johnson's administration. It was impossible for Sam to take his job seriously. Moreover, the reception of his articles based on the trip abroad encouraged him to believe that he could earn a living with his pen. Both the *Alta California* and the *Enterprise* begged for more articles. The *Chicago Tribune* also wanted contributions and the *New York Tribune*, edited by the famous Horace Greeley, calmly placed Mark on the staff as a free-lance writer. Magazines urged him to submit sketches and he received eighteen invitations to lecture. Even James Gordon Bennett, editor of the *New York Herald*, asked him to be a correspondent for his paper.

While he was considering or refusing these surprising offers, Sam received the most important letter of all. It was from Elisha Bliss, Jr., of the American Publishing Company in Hartford, Connecticut. Mr. Clemens was told that if he "had any thought of writing a book or could be induced to do so" Mr. Bliss would like to see him at once. Although Sam wrote an immediate reply he received no answer, because, as he learned later, Bliss was ill. So it was with all decisions hanging in air that Sam dashed off to spend Christmas with the New York man he had met on his trip abroad.

The festivities began with a dinner party of four. Two other *Quaker City* shipmates completed the quartet and one of them was Charley Langdon from Elmira. They exchanged reminiscences until they were weak with laughter.

As Charles Langdon was leaving he said to Sam, "My father and sister are down from Elmira, staying at the St. Nicholas Hotel, and I'd like very much to have you meet them—if you have time."

"Your sister Olivia?" exclaimed Sam. "The girl of the miniature? Why, Charley, I'd cancel any engagement for the privilege of meeting her."

So two days before Christmas Sam was presented to Miss Olivia Langdon and her father, Mr. Jervis Langdon. They had invited him to dinner. At first Sam was overcome by finding the actual young lady even lovelier than her portrait, but Mr. Langdon soon drew him out. Sam's dry comments on the trip and on the great West, as he knew it, kept the three Langdons laughing all through the meal. He was quite aware that Olivia was quietly studying him, as if he were the oddest creature she had ever met.

After dinner the Langdons took their guest to Steinway Hall, where Charles Dickens was to read scenes from his books. Dickens, appearing in a black velvet jacket, with a bright red flower in his buttonhole, proved to be a consummate actor. When he read the scene in *David Copperfield* picturing Steerforth's death in the great storm, Sam, sitting beside Olivia, saw her surreptitiously wipe her eyes and longed to comfort her.

As he lay sleepless that night, thinking over the party, awesome adjectives about the Langdons crossed his mind. Wealthy, elegant, conservative, cultured—they were all that. They must, of course, regard him as crude and un-

polished. It was intoxicating, therefore, to be invited by
Olivia to call on New Year's Day at a friend's house where
she was receiving. Charley took him there at eleven in the
morning and they stayed until midnight.

The fashionable callers, many of whom had read his
Tribune articles and also *The Jumping Frog,* seemed to
find the Langdons' odd friend vastly entertaining. Sam's
own attention was given to Olivia. His eyes followed her
every move. He listened for every word spoken in that soft,
sweet voice. Never had he met so graceful, charming, and
exquisite a young woman.

Only one other occasion during his stay in New York
could compare with the New Year's reception. This was a
dinner party given by the most famous preacher in the
country, Henry Ward Beecher. His daughter, Harriet
Beecher Stowe, was one of the brilliant assemblage. As he
shook the small hand which had written *Uncle Tom's
Cabin,* Sam's thoughts flew back to Cincinnati, where the
Beecher family had left such a deep impression, and still
farther back to his own rage at what he considered the
book's violent injustice to most Southern planters. Tonight such emotions seemed far away. He was completely
captivated by the sparkling conversation at the dinner
table. The party, however, had one great fault. Olivia
Langdon was not there.

On his return to his absurd secretarial job, Mark found
Washington very gay. He was invited here and there and
was persuaded to make two speeches, one at the Corre-

spondents' Club. Yet the capital seemed to him so corroded by sordid and unscrupulous personal ambition that real sociability did not exist. Suddenly his depression was lifted by a letter from Elisha Bliss, of the American Publishing Company. It asked Mark to come to Hartford to discuss the travel book he had proposed. Bliss wished him to sign a contract at once. Mark liked the breezy vitality of the editor and was impressed by the choice he was offered between accepting ten thousand dollars outright or waiting for royalties from the sale. Inexperienced as he was, Mark consulted Henry Ward Beecher before deciding. On his advice he settled for royalties. Hurrying back to Washington, he turned his back on all frivolities and began to write with furious concentration.

It was interrupted by bad news from Bliss. It seemed that the publishers of *Alta California* had copyrighted Mark's letters with the intention of bringing them out as a book. Mark had to go out to California in order to solve the difficulty. Colonel John McComb, editor in chief of the newspaper, who had from the first disagreed with its owners, supported Mark's right to use his own material for a book. Other friendly editors in San Francisco lent their influence also. The *Alta* finally gave way and Mark was free to go ahead with his book for the American Publishing Company.

With the problem solved, Mark went on an extended lecture tour through the West. To see all his old friends again and once more earn goodly sums of money was exhilarating. In spite of lectures, gay parties, and tiresome trips, he managed to go on writing. By the time he returned to the East in late July, he had a finished manuscript to place in the hands of Elisha Bliss.

Surely such accomplishment deserved a reward, he said to himself. Ingeniously he managed to wangle an invitation to visit the Langdon family in Elmira. When Charley met the train he shot a horrified glance at the wanderer from the wild West. "You have other clothes with you, Mark, I hope," he burst out. Without rancor Mark answered soothingly that his bag contained a fine outfit. The next morning he was cordially welcomed at the big hospitable home on the square.

Mr. Jervis Langdon and his elder daughter, Mrs. Theodore Crane, seemed delighted to see him. So did Mr. Crane. Mrs. Langdon was gently courteous. And Olivia was just that and nothing more. After a day or two of unavailing efforts to lure her into personal conversation, Mark said to Charley with a sigh, "I suppose your sister Livy, as you call her, thinks you are entertaining a tornado. It sometimes dawns upon me that I talk too much."

Charley's grunt carried eloquent assent and the look he turned on his guest was one of warning. It was evident to him and, indeed, to all the Langdons that Sam was falling in love with their beautiful, precious, and saintly Olivia. Jervis Langdon and the Cranes were obviously untroubled by the situation, but the others were in a panic. Their attitude convinced Mark that his case was hopeless and he decided to flee.

Much relieved, Charley planned to go with him to the train. In a flutter of farewells the two climbed into the stylish two-seated open cart behind the coachman. The horse sprang forward with a violent jerk and the rear seat, insecurely fastened, slid out, dumping the two occupants on the cobblestone drive.

For a moment Mark lay dazed. Charles, scrambling to his feet, stooped over him. "Are you hurt, Mark?"

"I guess not—not too badly," he muttered weakly, "but I do feel . . . very . . . very queer." His closed eyes gave no hint of his sudden inspiration.

Half-carried to the house by Charley and the butler, he sank limply into a chair. Mr. and Mrs. Langdon and Olivia hovered around him. He was put to bed at once, and later Olivia herself brought him a cup of hot tea. A murmured word of thanks, a sigh, a stifled groan as he shifted the pillows indicated patient suffering. Next day he bravely declared he intended to take the afternoon train. No one but Charley would hear of such a thing. Livy, full of concern, spent hours cheering him. He responded gratefully, but made little effort to talk. Without one qualm of conscience Sam spent two marvelous weeks recovering and left Elmira determined to win the only girl he had ever loved.

As 1868 advanced Mark Twain once more plunged into lecturing. His engagements were arranged by James Redpath of Boston, the outstanding agent for celebrities, who had sought this Western favorite ever since he returned from the Holy Land. Choosing for his theme, "Vandals Abroad," Mark was sent out on a long tour of the Middle

West. It proved immensely successful and everywhere newspapers gave the lecture warm notices.

Whenever Mark spoke at a town near Elmira, he hastened to the Langdon house on the square. Every visit drew him closer to Olivia, the Cranes, and the head of the household. On one of these occasions Sam tremulously asked Mr. Langdon for "his daughter's hand," according to the custom of the period. Given permission to speak to Olivia herself, he received only the shy answer, "Ah, please, give me time to think about it." Before the year's end, however, he had won her consent to a secret and tentative engagement. Her father then requested Sam to submit a list of persons who knew him well enough to report on his character.

As he journeyed to Pittsburgh, Cleveland, Chicago, and at last to St. Louis, where he was engulfed once more in family affection, he wrote romantic letters to Olivia, penned with ardor and hope. At the end of January, 1869, he reached Elmira again, in wild impatience to hear his fate.

Closeted in Mr. Langdon's study, the young man trembled before the grave look turned upon him. He learned then that the men Mark had chosen to speak for him had all agreed that in spite of Mark Twain's brilliance, which would assure a glamorous career, Sam Clemens, the man, would make a very poor husband. "Haven't you any friends who believe in your character?" asked Olivia's father.

"Yes," was the reply, spoken in a low tone, "but I wanted you to have an unbiased judgment. You see, my close friends would lie for me."

At this Mr. Langdon leaned forward with outstretched hand. "Well, I am your friend anyway," he said. "I know you and believe in you."

It was a cloudy day, but for Sam the room suddenly filled with sunshine. He knew that with her father's approval established, he could persuade the girl of his heart to take the risk of accepting him. The engagement was announced on the fourth of February.

The following weeks of Sam's stay were made still more radiant by the arrival of the proofs of his travel book. Hour by hour Olivia went over them with him. He was grateful for her occasional improvements of his English and the elimination of certain extravagant expressions. She laughed gaily at the right places, and if some of the comic incidents failed to amuse her, if she raised her eyebrows over a daring description, respect for the writer's freedom silenced any suggestion of change.

Delightedly the author said, "What wonderful good fortune that I'm going to have a good editor as my wife."

Innocents Abroad, or the New Pilgrim's Progress was published in July of that year. Sam had dedicated it to his "Ancient Mother," then fifty-nine years old. In a month more than 5000 copies had been sold. The bold originality of the author's realism and his eloquent portrayal of the significant and the beautiful brought praise from most of

America's influential critics. Some modern readers, who find the ludicrous passages too juvenile and too lengthy, must realize that Mark's drollery was vastly superior to the clumsy humor of other nineteenth-century writers.

Sam had earned more than eight thousand dollars from his lectures, and his book was swiftly increasing his fame and fortune. Yet he still considered himself more a journalist than an author and told Mr. Langdon that he wanted a newspaper connection. He felt that he should not carry Olivia too far from her doting family and he said so. In the end Jervis Langdon bought for him a one-third interest in the *Buffalo Express* and in the middle of August he began work as contributor and editor.

He did not keep at it very long, however. He was anxious to accumulate enough money to impress his future father-in-law. Off he went on another lecture tour. This time Redpath sent him all over New England. "I'm deathly afraid of those intellectual Yankees," he confessed to Livy, as he started off. "I don't think they'll be interested in my tales of pioneer life in the West." Nevertheless, the tour was a financial success and in Boston he made many new friends, chief of whom was William Dean Howells, a writer who was assistant editor of the *Atlantic Monthly*.

In a joyous mood Mark returned to Elmira to await the wedding, which was set for the evening of February 2, 1870. That very morning the postman added an unexpected sparkle to the occasion by bringing him a check for

$4000 from his publisher. The minister who was to perform the ceremony had already won Sam's admiration. Brother of the more famous Henry Ward Beecher, the Reverend Thomas K. Beecher was the liberal, unorthodox minister of the Park Congregational Church, which stood just opposite the Langdons' old-fashioned mansion on the square. He had spent many sociable hours with Mark, who appreciated the wide influence Beecher had achieved in the entire region as an exponent of social justice and freedom of thought.

A little after seven o'clock that evening some hundred privileged friends gathered in the Langdons' spacious parlors for the simple ceremony. Everyone agreed that Olivia had never looked more beautiful. As Samuel Langhorne Clemens claimed his bride with the traditional kiss, he whispered, "Livy, this is forever."

CHAPTER · · · · · · · · NINE

Life in Buffalo began for Sam with a stunning surprise on the night after the wedding. A large party, including the Langdons and the Beechers, escorted the bride and groom from Elmira to Buffalo by train. Langdon's business associates there, who had been asked to find a pleasant boardinghouse for the Clemenses, met the train with a fleet of sleighs. Sam thought the drive through the city's streets would never end. When they finally stopped before a brilliantly lighted house and he saw two servants rush out to carry in the luggage, he wondered what kind of boarding place it could be.

In a daze he was led through handsomely decorated rooms. "It's our own home, dear!" Olivia explained exultingly. "Father gave it to us, and everything in it!"

Such was the fabulous prelude to a happy winter. In late spring, however, Olivia's father became ill and grew steadily worse. In June the Clemenses were called to Elmira to help nurse him. Taking turns through the day and night, Olivia, Mrs. Crane, and Sam took care of him until the August day when Jervis Langdon died. In a state of sorrow and exhaustion, Sam and Olivia returned to Buffalo, only to suffer another calamity. A dear friend of Livy's was stricken with typhoid fever while paying a visit to her and died in a few weeks. Too frail to bear this added strain, Olivia had to spend many weeks in bed.

Sam felt thrown completely out of gear by these distressing events. He said to his associate editor on the *Express*, "How on earth can a man write amid such an avalanche of woes?"

"The answer is, you do, Mark," was the reply.

Indeed, Mark's pen somehow kept busy with editorials for his paper and sketches for a new magazine which Elisha Bliss of Hartford was starting. Moreover, after several impractical ideas had been abandoned, he had accepted a suggestion of Bliss's for a new book. It was to be a complete story of Mark's years in the Far West. The publisher was eager for a follow-up of *Innocents Abroad*, to increase its sales.

Mark was flattered to have his first book published in England and translated into several languages on the continent, but Bliss was not. He knew that foreign publication yielded nothing but prestige. There were no international copyright laws to protect an author and nothing was paid to either writer or publisher. This dishonest practice was called pirating. Only the American market profited American publishers. Sam was vague about the situation, but he started to write his Western tale, *Roughing It*.

It was not money that he was concerned about just then. *Innocents Abroad* went on selling at the rate of several thousand copies a month and hardly a day went by without personal calls and letters praising the book. What troubled him and therefore made it hard for him to write was Olivia's lack of strength. In November a baby boy was born, and named Langdon. He had arrived before he was due and his extreme delicacy dimmed his father's joy in having a son.

Buffalo began to seem to the Clemenses a place of sorrow and anxiety. They had few friends there, and by April they decided to leave. Sam arranged to have the house sold and he also sold, at considerable loss, his share in the *Buffalo Express*. While they were considering a move to Hartford, which offered congenial literary associations, they accepted Mrs. Crane's invitation to spend the summer at her country place, Quarry Farm. In this spacious home, with a glorious view of the hills and valleys around Elmira, strength returned to Olivia and Sam struggled earnestly to get on with his memoirs of Nevada and California.

One morning he excitedly waved a letter before his wife's eyes. "It's from Joe Goodman, my old editor of the Virginia City *Enterprise*. He's coming East. Livy, this is a windfall for me. Joe is a good editor and he can tell me whether I'm on the right track with my book. I know you and your sister will like him. May I invite him to come here?"

Of course he was told that his friends would be welcome. Any doubts concerning a man from the untamed West vanished when the charming and handsome young editor appeared.

Before a week of Goodman's visit had passed, Mark asked him to read the finished chapters of his book and give an absolutely frank opinion of them. There was no use in wasting time on a worthless piece of work, said Mark. Goodman settled down with the manuscript, while Mark pretended to write letters. With mounting uneasiness he watched Goodman turn page after page. So passed an hour of complete silence.

Suddenly Mark shouted, "I knew this yarn was rot. Don't bother to read any more of it. You just don't want to tell me how bad it is."

Joe looked up in surprise. "Why, Mark, you're crazy. Where's your judgment? I've been absolutely absorbed. It's a true picture of life in the West. It's exciting and funny and real. I like it better than *Innocents Abroad*. Go right ahead, you talented old buzzard. You'll have another big success."

Although his face lighted up, Sam couldn't believe what he had heard. Joe had to reassure him several times. Once convinced, however, he took up his work with such zest that often he dashed off sixty pages in a single day. His consequent radiance poured over the household. Whenever he coaxed the baby to smile and play peekaboo, he would say, "Isn't he beautiful, Livy darling? Isn't this the loveliest summer?"

Sure now that he could finish the book by fall, he signed another contract with Redpath for a lecture tour. Although Olivia was opposed to the plan, she said no word against it. He explained that he had to make up for his loss in selling his share in the *Buffalo Express*. "Olivia Langdon's husband," he said, "must measure up to her father's expectations—and her own."

Olivia smiled sympathetically. Having always taken wealth for granted, she merely thought it natural that a man who had known poverty so long now found it exciting to pile up money. What she was unable to grasp was the bad effect this kind of ambition could have upon a creative writer.

It was necessary now for Sam to go to Hartford to look for a house. The house he found was fairly small, but pleasant, and in September they moved in and engaged servants and a nurse for the baby. Olivia liked all her husband's new friends: the Twichells, the Blisses, Harriet Beecher Stowe and her husband, and Charles Dudley Warner, a writer and an assistant editor of the *Hartford Courier*. But it was hard that Sam must start off on his lecture tour before they had time to enjoy the place together.

He had divided feelings about lecturing. He hated the boredom of train travel, the packing and unpacking, and the gamble he had to take at every hotel in the matter of bathroom, service, and food. On the other hand, he enjoyed the drama of holding his audience, making people laugh and applaud.

His manner of slipping across the stage and gravely introducing himself with exaggerated praise was irresistibly funny. His bushy hair and spread-eagle mustache and the twinkling eyes under formidable eyebrows achieved a perfect comedy effect. He acted, rather than read, and he developed to a high degree the entertainer's art. In most towns and cities this was recognized with enthusiasm. In New England, however, the audiences failed to appreciate his quality; they accepted him merely as an amusing eccentric.

What he liked best about engagements near Boston were the hours between performances which he spent with other members of the Redpath circuit. The humorists, Josh Billings and Petroleum Nasby, so enjoyed by President Lincoln, were his special pals. Bret Harte also turned up, famous now for his short stories and his book, *The Luck of Roaring Camp*. Easteners did not realize how unreal were his well-told tales. But William Dean Howells made no such mistake. He considered Mark Twain the most important writer in the country and eagerly sought his companionship. Thomas Bailey Aldrich, editor of a literary magazine, was also a member of this group.

Practically every day Sam wrote love letters to his wife. He knew she was too shy to adjust easily to a new environment. Whenever possible he paid a visit to Hartford, and in March, 1872, he joined her at the Langdon home in Elmira, where a little girl was born, a strong, healthy baby whom they named Susan. For nearly three months happiness reigned in the Clemens family. But once again fate struck a cruel blow. Fragile little Langdon died after a brief illness.

Both parents were inconsolable. Sam not only suffered grief, but anguished guilt. One windy afternoon he had taken Langdon for a drive. Absorbed in thought about his book, he had failed to notice that the warm rug wrapped around the child had slipped to the carriage floor. Next day Langdon had a very high fever and the terrified father believed that what appeared to be a dangerous cold had resulted from his carelessness. Although doctors soon diagnosed the sickness as diphtheria, Sam was never convinced.

In strange contrast with this dark shadow was the shining triumph of *Roughing It*, Mark's book about Western pioneering. It won high praise from reviewers and 40,000 copies were sold in its first three months. At last this brought him the realization that authorship was his true vocation. Accordingly, he began to consider carefully the income he must earn from books.

"You know, Livy," he said one day, "you and I have been proud as peacocks to have my *Innocents* brought out in England and *The Jumping Frog*, too. But it has dawned on me how unfair it is for them to refuse to share the returns with the author and the American publisher. It's a plain steal. If I'm going to depend for a living on writing books, they must earn money abroad as well as here. There are no copyright laws to protect us. But we think we've found an honest publisher in England who will bring out *Roughing It* and pay royalties on it. Still, I think I'd better go to London and size up this new publisher, Routledge."

"Go to England?" Olivia's tone was plaintive. "Oh, Sam, you're always leaving me." Before he could answer, however, she caught his hand and said quickly, "Of course, you must go, dear. It's important to your career to assure your just share. With my little Susy for company, I'll be all right."

Sam sailed in August. The very morning he reached London, he took a cab to the Routledge publishing company. Members of the staff were at luncheon and cordially invited him to join them. The instant he began to talk in his soft drawl and relate racy incidents, the listeners were completely enthralled. They wouldn't let him go and finally carried him off to dinner at the Savage Club.

There the party was joined by Henry Irving, the noted Shakespearean actor, and by Henry M. Stanley, recently returned from his famous sojourn with David Livingstone in Africa. Other celebrities added themselves to the group. Accepting them all in his casual way, Mark was aware that the British were ready to enjoy an American oddity.

That first day, so incredibly packed with sociability, was only a beginning. For three months Mark Twain was lionized by writers, artists, journalists, and even a few titled aristocrats who liked to dip into Bohemia. He was obliged to speak at banquets and his speeches were reported in full. Even his little quips were quoted far and wide. At one exclusive luncheon the man who introduced him remarked that here was a true representative of the American people—the only people in the world who carried cotton umbrellas. "Yes," retorted Mark, "I always carry a cotton umbrella, because that is the only kind that an Englishman won't steal."

Occasionally, as he stood before some august assemblage, he would wonder how the boy from Hannibal, the typesetter who slept on the floor, the penniless mining prospector, the reporter paid twenty-five dollars a week, happened to be acclaimed by these cultured British sophisticates.

At last, glutted with entertainment, filled to the brim with the beauty of England, he bade good-by to his host of new friends. Before he left he had had printed in the *Spectator* a letter denouncing the act of the English publisher who had pirated his first two books as a shameful violation of justice.

The homeward voyage provided an exciting episode. During a fearful storm a wrecked freight barge was sighted, with nine men desperately clinging to it. Immediately the captain called for volunteers to save them. The ship was stopped, a lifeboat was lowered and a picked crew from the many volunteers set forth over the gigantic waves. Stand-

ing on the heaving deck in the rain, Sam watched the rescuers reach the barge and maneuver the half-drowned
seamen, one by one, into the lifeboat. It seemed hardly
possible that the heavily laden boat could be brought back
to the ship, but the feat was accomplished and at last the
rescued men and their rescuers were dripping on the deck.

Mark wrote a stirring account of the incident to be sent
to the Royal Humane Society of London. With it went a
petition, which he persuaded every passenger to sign, that
medals be presented to the heroes. Later he learned that
this had been done and the men had won national recognition.

Mark's was a happy home-coming. Olivia was well and
baby Susan more adorable than ever. All the Hartford
neighbors, of course, gave him a hearty welcome. When
Livy learned that in spite of Redpath's plea, Mark was not
going to make a lecture tour that year, she was radiant.
Now that he was at home, she was ready to entertain all
the members of the literary circle. Since the house was too
small for parties, she couldn't invite them all at once and
she had to keep the occasions simple.

Mark had been making up his mind to change all this.
To his surprise, a timid suggestion that they might build
a large, comfortable house was applauded by his wife.
They had a fine time driving about to find the proper site.
At last they discovered it, a wooded tract of land overlooking the valley and the hills. There was even a brook wind-
ing through it.

The huge tract was bought and an architect engaged to design the house of their desire. Mark outlined the absolute essentials: a very large living room, plenty of bedrooms with baths, a study for himself and, on the third floor, a billiard room for his recreation. At the rear the house had to have a wide verandah from which they could enjoy the lovely hills. "Just an American version of a castle," he said, "but worthy of a Langdon."

Thus began the year 1873. Soon Mark was involved in a job of writing that was a complete departure for him. He was collaborating on a novel with Charles Dudley Warner. Olivia hoped that the New Englander would curb her husband's exuberant style. Joe Twichell said, "How on earth can two writers so utterly different in background and temperament ever work together?"

But they did. The tale was set in Washington. Warner handled the love theme and outlined the quite incredible plot. Mark seized his chance to scourge the worship of power and money which was undermining Congress. One of his humorous characters became a legend. Colonel Sellers, a penniless optimist, always certain that fame and fortune were just around the corner, was a kindhearted old dreamer, an absurd, lovable, gullible grown-up child who innocently aided some of the worst rascals in the government. In three months the book was finished and sent to the American Publishing Company, entitled *The Gilded Age*.

In May, leaving the supervision of the new house's con-

struction to the architect, the Clemenses set sail for England, with little Susy and Livy's best friend, Miss Clara Spaulding. On the first morning of their stay in the large, comfortable English hotel suite, the two ladies noted with interest that the journals reported the arrival of Mark Twain as an outstanding event. Before the day was over several people had called and by the end of the week the suite's private parlor seethed with visitors. Knowing how unprepared Clara and Livy were for the proud names brought up by the bellboy, Mark delighted in surprising them.

"Look who's clamoring to see us now!" he said one afternoon, handing Clara a card.

She gasped. "Not really! Robert Browning! Why, how on earth—"

Mark finished the sentence for her—"could he think this barbarian worthy of his notice? Well, you know, he's master of the incomprehensible."

Another day brought an invitation to a luncheon given in Mark's honor by the outstanding English philosopher, Herbert Spencer. This time it was Olivia's turn to splutter. "Listen to him, Clara, saying, 'How nice!' He's absolutely incapable of awe!"

"I deny the charge," Mark retorted. "Mont Blanc awed me. The British Museum awes me. When Susy took her first steps I was in a frenzy of awe. I'm grateful for all this English friendliness and I don't understand it. But . . . . Well, people are just people even if they're famous."

At impressive dinner parties at private houses Mark was

not so casual. He put his whole mind on selecting the right forks for fish and game. Whenever he caught his wife's anxious eye, he conscientiously divided attention evenly between the ladies on each side of him. At a luncheon party given by the clergyman-author, Charles Kingsley, after Mark had pretended he'd never read one of Kingsley's books, he broke into his host's laughter by saying that he knew *Water Babies* by heart, considered it a work of genius, and, together with millions of children, loved and admired it.

The constant round of entertainment finally exhausted Olivia. Sam whisked her away to a small hotel in Edinburgh. There they made just one friend, the doctor he summoned for his wife. He was John Brown, author of *Rab and His Friends,* a well-loved dog story. The charming Scotchman proved such a good physician that Olivia was soon well enough to survive several visits to beautiful country homes, another exciting fortnight in London, and a trip to Paris for sight-seeing and shopping. Then she was quite ready to go home.

Susy, spoiled by admiring guests, was not ready. Neither was her father. He had promised to give a few lectures in London under the auspices of the manager of Charles Dickens' tours. With some English friends, Olivia and Clara Spaulding attended the first lecture. As they gazed around the hall, the biggest in London, they agreed that they had never seen a larger or more fashionable audience. Olivia was nervous until she heard the hearty applause as her husband strolled out on the platform and the laughter following every drawled, humorous comment of his.

As the applause at the end of the lecture finally subsided, Clara murmured, "Well, Livy, this ovation teaches me that America still underestimates your husband. The British think he's a genius."

For five nights and one matinee the big hall was filled. Mark had to give his word to the highly gratified agent that he would come back for a return engagement as soon as he had escorted his party home. Accordingly, after a month's absence, he was again entertaining London audiences and giving after-dinner speeches at distinguished gatherings. Old friendships were renewed and new acquaintances charmed into friends.

In mid-January, 1874, Sam boarded a steamer for New York. Since at that time most vessels took two weeks to cross the ocean, he had plenty of time for contemplation as he lay in his deck chair swathed in rugs, with the wintry sun in his face.

What were his thoughts then? A tantalizing mystery clings to any famous person who has slipped off the inevitable mask worn for public appearance. Mark's deliberate disguise on the platform was unaffected simplicity without pretense of either elegance or depth of culture. He knew that was what his public wanted—especially in England. There was never a hint that beneath his humor and robust enjoyment of life lay an equally powerful melancholy, a skeptical view of existence.

To him the struggles, sorrows, and disappointments he had both observed and experienced were inexplicable. What was the meaning of pain, he had always wondered. Still more inexplicable was the cruel, selfish, hypocritical behavior of human beings. He often cursed his own burden of guilt.

Nevertheless, it is impossible to believe that at this moment of his life Mark Twain could pursue grim meditations very long. Wasn't he on top of his world? He had wanted to make money, and it was flowing toward him in golden streams. The only woman he had ever loved was his wife, and they had a delightful child. He had established himself as a writer and speaker both at home and abroad. His admirers were legion and he could count on many solid friendships. There on the good ship *Parthia* he must have admitted that life had turned out better than he had dreamed it could.

There was only one tickle of doubt in his mind. Would it go on like this? But when he reached Hartford again and felt Olivia's arms about him, the question perished in a blaze of gratitude and happiness.

CHAPTER · · · · · · · TEN

No tarnish dimmed the bright, leisurely days of the next year. Mark wrote a comedy around his famous character, Colonel Sellers, and as it played to crowded houses around the country Mark's bank account increased month by month. He pretended to share Olivia's fearfulness over the cost of the house and made much of his earnings from the theater.

One day when William Dean Howells was visiting the family, the butler, George, who was a sly diplomat, brought the mail to the luncheon table. Mark picked out a certain card at once and cried, "Here's the latest report from my theatrical manager. I made a hundred dollars from the performance two nights ago and one hundred and fifty last night!" Flinging down his napkin, he marched around the room triumphantly waving the card.

"Did you ever see such a child?" laughed Olivia. "Anyone would think he lived to amass money. What he really likes is to spend it."

Howells, who was now editor in chief of the *Atlantic Monthly*, had proof of Mark's unworldly side. He accepted for the first time a short story from him, for which he paid forty dollars. Mark, feeling that he had received the literary accolade, was prouder of appearing in the *Atlantic* than of anything he had yet published. The two men often exchanged visits and at dinner parties in Boston Mark was the center of interest even when Ralph Waldo Emerson was present.

In the summer the Clemenses settled down again at Mrs. Crane's home, Quarry Farm. One June day a dark-haired baby girl was born, and named Clara in honor of Miss Spaulding. In the octagonal summerhouse which Mrs. Crane had built for her brother-in-law at the farm on the very brink of a lofty ridge, a great literary creation was germinating. Tom Sawyer and Huckleberry Finn were emerging from the realm of imagination to set out upon their immortal careers. In order to bring them into the world their creator relived his own boyhood and to do so brought him the most glorious hours he had ever spent at his desk.

Once again he was devising pranks and undertaking risky adventures on the Mississippi River with his gang. All day, from half past eight in the morning until five in the afternoon, Sam Clemens dwelt in Hannibal, Missouri. On its dusty streets he met the boys and girls he used to know, sat rebelliously on his bench at school, and prowled with his companions through the vast, mysterious cave. Best of all was to go back with them to Glassocks Island. To recall those marvelous days of sunshine and those nights beside the campfire inspired his writing with sheer magic.

To Olivia's frequent protest that he was working too hard, Sam would reply, "But it isn't work, Livy. I often feel that I'm simply taking dictation from some outside source. This writing is fun, splendid fun. The incidents just pour themselves out."

Then suddenly the flow stopped. Why, he didn't know. Somehow, he was not much disturbed. He quietly laid aside the manuscript to await another surge of inspiration. By fall the long-expected news came that they could move into the Hartford house. To be sure, it was not completely finished. Sam regaled relatives and friends with exaggerated accounts of the frightful hullabaloo made by carpenters, plumbers, decorators, and landscape gardeners. But in due time the grounds were perfected, and lavishly furnished rooms were ready for private enjoyment and for the welcoming of friends.

Sam never ceased to revel in the gasp of amazed admiration breathed by each guest on first entering the fabulous house. He loved to answer questions from critics of unconventional architecture. To the query, "Why was the house placed at right angles to the street?" he replied, "To get the best view from both the front and the rear windows." "But then you had to put the kitchen facing the street, didn't you?" This won the solemn answer, "Oh, dear no! We could have put it somewhere else. But we did this so that the servants could see the circus parades without having to rush out on the front lawn."

In his new study Sam had a strange invention, a machine called a typewriter. He used it until his patience wore out. Then he began to swear at the mistakes made by the clumsy, noisy machine, and gladly returned to the gentle submissiveness of a pen.

The pen was busy during the winter of 1875. Howells was enthusiastic about Mark's idea of writing for the *Atlantic Monthly* a series of articles on the great river which had been such an integral part of his youth. Its fantastic behavior, as observed from a steamer's pilothouse, was presented with vividness, humor, and authenticity of detail. The articles were snatched up by newspapers all over the continent. Even though the newspapers paid nothing, the articles kept the writer's prestige mounting in Canada as well as in his own country.

It was doubtless such thieving as this which impelled Mark to write a piece on the need of copyright laws. To his wife's surprise, he also published articles in favor of suffrage for women. As spring advanced, however, he was once more drawn to the Hannibal boys and life on the Mississippi as it used to be. His ear caught the voices once so familiar—the soft cadence of Negro speech, the harsh dialect of lumbermen and stevedores, the picturesque, un-grammatical language characteristic of the region. This time he was not merely taking dictation from his memory. He was constructing a story that would give direction to the exciting incidents bound to happen to intrepid and inventive boys.

"That life in Hannibal was freedom," Mark sighed to Olivia one day, "blissful freedom, in spite of poverty and sorrow and the shock of discovering evil and cruelty. Why can't human beings go on being free? They don't!"

At first startled, then moved, Olivia answered tenderly, "I suppose it's because we get entangled in material cares and in relationships—friends, babies, people we love. Children live in a world of their own, outside responsibilities, don't they?"

"Yes," mused her husband, "they are monsters of egotism, the lucky dogs!"

When Olivia edited the finished book, she deleted a number of Huck Finn's swear words. The excision was approved by Howells, to whom Mark sent the manuscript. Olivia's doubt about the value of the story had shaken his confidence in it, but his friend restored it by this comment: "It is altogether the best boy's story I ever read. It will be an immense success, but I think you ought to treat it explicitly as a boy's story; grownups will enjoy it just as much if you do, and if you should put it forth as a study of boy character from the grown-up point of view you give the wrong key to it."

Even with this encouragement Mark kept working on

the book for some time and it was not published until December, 1876. *The Adventures of Tom Sawyer* brought the author countless letters of praise. Youngsters loved the mischievous inventions of Tom and his followers. Adults found in the tale an enchanted presentation of the childhood which everyone had wanted. "This book is ageless and will live forever," commented one distinguished critic.

Relaxed and happy in this glow of success, Sam devoted himself that winter to enjoyment of home, family, and close friends. He invented games to amuse Susy, paid visits to Boston, and in his spacious third-floor quarters indulged his mania for billiards whenever he could persuade someone to play with him. He wrote short stories and humorous bits for newspapers and magazines when the mood seized him. A book of sketches published the year before had proved a failure from every standpoint. But what did that matter to an author so famous that a letter from abroad addressed to "Mark Twain, God Knows Where" actually reached him?

All his spare time was devoted to English history in the sixteenth century. For some time he had secretly cherished the idea of creating a story about an English prince who, disguised beyond recognition, lived for a time among the poorest and wickedest of his subjects. After long study Sam chose for his hero the son of Henry VIII, the prince who became King of England as Edward VI. All summer was devoted to writing the tale, but finally he locked it in his desk.

Early in the spring of 1878 the Clemens family, with Clara Spaulding and the children's nurse, sailed for Europe. After traveling in Germany, they toured through much of Italy. In August Sam left them there in order to take a walking trip through Switzerland with Joe Twichell, who came over as his guest. The purpose of this jaunt was to gather material for another travel book. In Munich, where the family settled for the winter, Mark began it, but with no enthusiasm.

One night at dinner, he growled to Livy and Clara, "Well, I've torn up everything I've written so far. The Alps are to blame. How puny one feels in their awful presence."

Happy and sociable were the spring sojourns in Paris and London, but the Clemenses were glad to reach Quarry Farm for the summer. Mark had to force himself to finish *A Tramp Abroad*. He knew his humor was not spontaneous, but he enjoyed burlesquing the German language and certainly his extremely funny essay upon it reflects his enjoyment. Morever, many of his descriptions of scenery are superb. Once the book was shipped off, he plunged joyfully back into sixteenth-century England, a period crammed with excitement and profound changes. As he finished the story at Hartford, he read his chapters aloud to the children before the fire on winter evenings. Even six-year-old Clara listened with absorption.

Susy thought her father the most delightful and bewildering creature in the world. Her one complaint was the rule that only severe sickness excused anyone from appearing at the breakfast table, where he indulged in jokes and lively talk no matter how sleepy and unresponsive the audience was. Susy made it plain that this was very trying.

In July, 1880, a third little daughter joined the family. Her father wrote Joe Twichell that little Jean was "the comeliest and daintiest and perfectest little creature the continents and archipelagoes have seen since Clara and Susy were her size."

That fall Mark took a dip into politics. Senator James A. Garfield of Ohio was running for President and Ex-president Grant was to speak for him in Hartford. Local members of the Republican party, who knew that Mark had met Grant several times and admired him greatly, persuaded him to make two welcoming speeches for the hero. The sly jokes embroidering these long-remembered speeches made even the solemn General smile broadly. It was typical of the ceaseless hospitality of the Clemenses that they gave a luncheon for some of the visitors. Mr. Fred Grant, the General's son, was an especially welcome guest.

Having finished the book which he entitled *The Prince and the Pauper*, Mark decided to publish it by means of a peculiar arrangement with his friend James R. Osgood. Mark undertook all the expense of illustrating, editing, and printing the book. Osgood was to handle the work, and organize the sales. For this he was to receive seven and one half per cent of the profits and Mark was to have all the rest. It was published in December, 1881.

Sales of this imaginative and stirring story went slowly. Readers were unprepared for such a book from the humorist's pen. They did not understand the fantasy or realize its moral beauty. The efforts made by the boys—prince and pauper alike—to better conditions for the poor and revoke unjust laws add purpose to the sweep of action. In time the story, glowing with the author's passionate feeling for human justice, made its way into the hearts of young and old.

Between sharing responsibilities with Osgood, Mark had been working on a story about Huckleberry Finn, who took Tom Sawyer's place as chief hero. Once more he was basking in the hot sunshine of Hannibal and thrilling to Huck's journey on a raft with the runaway slave Jim, one of Mark's most appealing characters. Much as he loved writing it, he was not sure the book was good.

Olivia, consulted by her husband about the finished half of the tale, was still more unsure. "Well," she said, "I like *The Prince and the Pauper* better. Still you do make that period before the Civil War very vivid. Poor Huck is certainly very rough and ignorant, but he is appealing."

No creative artist could fail to be somewhat crushed by such a comment. Mark put the manuscript aside and busied himself with writing a few stories and sketches between club meetings, festivities, and absorbing family life. That he and Olivia were spending enormous sums failed to trouble him. Christmas topped all other occasions. From Christmas Eve, when he helped Olivia trim the gigantic

tree, until after New Year's the Clemenses held court. There was a round of children's parties with charades and theatricals acted by both children and parents. Sam loved dressing up and threw his whole soul into every part. Olivia, now more experienced and less shy, was a charming hostess. The spacious lamplit house, with crackling fires for coziness, itself created an atmosphere of good-fellowship.

"What will your next book be, Mark?" That was the question James Osgood insistently asked. It wasn't hard to decide that he might do a book on the Mississippi based to some extent on the articles published in the *Atlantic*.

That was a review of the past. A new look at the river was essential for a book. Together the two publishers went south in search of material.

At New Orleans they were entertained by George Cable, a writer whom Mark had met and liked when he was visiting in Hartford. When Joel Chandler Harris, author of the immortal Uncle Remus stories, joined the trio at Cable's house, Mark's pleasure was complete. Harris was shy and silent, but in the evening as the four men talked of life and literature, history and moral problems, he was lured into conversation and his stories produced laughter that rocked the house.

During the long journey up and down the Mississippi Mark spent most of his time as a visitor in the pilothouse. His first observation was startling. There were almost no boats of any kind on the river. Railroads had filched from it both freight and passengers. In his notebook Mark wrote, "The loneliness of this solemn, stupendous flood is impressive—and depressing."

The few steamers which were operating seemed luxurious compared with those of former days. All the ship's officers wore uniforms. New gadgets were installed in the pilothouse to increase efficiency. Beacon lights gave plain warning of rocks and reefs which Sam had once had to learn by heart. And strong headlights on the forecastle helped mightily in blazing the way through darkness and fog.

Sam made every effort to admire this progress. He said

to Osgood, "The river is far safer for travel and the steamers are far swifter than in my day, but, oh, Jim, there's no romance in piloting any more."

He was dumfounded to discover the vast changes made by the impetuous river itself. It had left high and dry, and completely out of sight, towns where Sam used to dock his ship. Former islands had joined the mainland. Others had been washed entirely away. Since the government had undertaken to pull out the dangerous snags so dreaded by pilots, much of the river's course was laid in new channels.

Mark's book, *Life on the Mississippi,* was published with much fanfare and ultimately brought him a fair profit from his original investment of $56,000. To fill the required two volumes, he had been obliged to pad his script with long stories and facts sure to be dated. But his vivid descriptions and riotously funny tales of his own training as a pilot gave the book high value as entertaining history.

The trip accomplished more than making this book possible. Mark returned from it with an irresistible urge to go on with his tale of Huckleberry Finn. He had to bide his time, but in the summer of 1883, at Quarry Farm, he plunged into the book again with his old zest and assurance.

It was such a happy summer, with his absorption in the book offset by joyous times with his three little girls, that he could forget financial worries. The Clemenses were spending more than their combined incomes justified.

Moreover, since he took no advice from experts, Sam made investments which were costly failures. He had put $32,000 into the manufacture of a steam pulley and had to watch it disappear. He had loaned a large sum to a friend to organize an insurance company, and it was years before the debt was paid back. His next project was a newly invented process of engraving. Taking a controlling interest in the patent, he engaged Charles L. Webster, the husband of his niece, to manage the business. Before its failure, this undertaking had consumed $40,000. He sorely needed ready cash.

"I'm going into the publishing business," he said to Olivia. "My experience with Osgood has shown me it is a lucrative affair. I'm training Charles Webster as a manager. He's really both energetic and intelligent."

Olivia had no wish to oppose this plan. But she wondered how her husband could stoke a fire fast enough to keep all his irons hot. He had been writing plays for some time. One that he wrote with Howells came very near to appearing on the stage. He invented a new game which he thought might be produced and sold to millions. Every few days he announced that he had a wonderful new idea for a story, and now and then he wrote and sold one. Meanwhile, he was completing his book about Huckleberry Finn, and of course there were always visitors to be entertained. For amusement he was apt to play billiards with some willing victim until the small hours of the morning, and he risked his neck by riding up and down the street on one of the high-wheeled bicycles fashionable at that time among the very young and brave.

By 1884 the Charles L. Webster Publishing Company was a reality, with an office in New York. The first book it issued was *The Adventures of Huckleberry Finn.* This was received with the kind of joy which meant excellent sales. Yet it had to wait many years for true appreciation. Beneath its humor lies a faithful and enduring picture of life before the Civil War in regions then on the edge of the great West. Nowadays the story is considered from every standpoint Mark Twain's most important artistic achievement. The distinguished critic, Bernard de Voto, for example, said of it: "No book has more of America in it, nor more delight. Like all great works of art, it is unique. All the world reads it for the first time."

Before the book was off the press, the author was once more whirling about the country on a lecture tour. He well knew it was the quickest way to make the money he needed to climb out of debt. Under the management of Major J. B. Ponds of Boston, he set off, but this time he was not alone. His new friend, George W. Cable, also experienced in lecturing, had joined him. They divided the program between them. Cable read from his books and sang songs of the old South. Mark told stories from his books and recounted incidents from his travels and adventures. He worked very hard to perfect these narratives and used no notes. The tour was a great success. Naturally each had some complaints of the other. Cable didn't like Mark's smoking and bursts of profanity. Mark detested Cable's stinginess and narrow piety. Yet they remained lifelong friends, if not intimates.

The trip afforded Sam a few cherished days at Keokuk, Iowa, where he saw not only Orion and his wife, but his mother, who was now living with Orion. At eighty-three, she still preserved her lighthearted manner and her strong likes and dislikes. After the lecture, which she proudly attended, Sam asked her if she could still dance. "Certainly can!" she responded, and sprang up to whisk about the room with the light, swift step of old.

Of course Mark spent the usual splendid Christmas in the Hartford house. The blazing fire, the joyous children, the friends and the fun, made it harder for him to return to the lecture platform. The tour continued until March, 1885. Its end brought no rest, however, for a tremendous publishing project was on the way.

It came about in an odd fashion on a night when Mark and Cable gave their program in New York at Steinway Hall. After the performance Olivia and her husband strolled out together into the foggy night. On the sidewalk several people were gathered around Richard Watson Gilder, the poet and editor of *Century Magazine*. The Clemenses joined them in time to hear Gilder say that at long last General Ulysses S. Grant had started to write his memoirs.

Sam made no comment until he and Olivia began walking with Gilder toward his house. There they discussed the publication of these memoirs. Gilder said he had heard that the Century Company had sent General Grant a contract. In the meantime *Century Magazine* had accepted three articles from the General for publication.

As the Clemenses parted from Gilder and walked on, Sam blurted out his fears about Grant's contract. "That innocent man won't get anything like the royalties he ought to have, Livy! Grant's memoirs! Why, they'll sell like Christmas cakes. The General is poor. He was robbed, you know, of all his savings by a villainous broker. He ought to ask a huge sum for his material. Livy, I'm going to go and tell Grant what his book is worth."

This he did the very next morning. The General's son Fred, who had become Mark's admiring friend, was present at the interview. His eyes nearly started from his head to learn that at least a quarter of a million copies of the memoirs were sure to be sold and that the author must have a fair share. Mark suggested that other publishers should be given a chance to bid for the memoirs. He wound up by declaring that as owner of the firm of Charles L. Webster he would gladly offer twenty per cent of all the profits.

For an instant Grant stared in amazement. Then with a slow shake of his massive head he replied, "But I couldn't accept such an offer, Mr. Clemens. It is nothing but philanthropy. Why, sir, the Century Company will not guarantee a sale of even 25,000 copies."

Snapping his fingers, snorting with disgust, Mark asserted that as an advance on royalties he would write out a check for $25,000 on the spot. Neither the General nor

Fred would decide the matter at once. But by the time Mark returned from his lecture tour they had collected enough information and advice to make up their minds to accept his offer.

This triumph was blighted by the shocking news that Grant had developed an incurable cancer of the throat. Nevertheless, he was bravely determined to finish his book, and the fact that he could earn enough from it to enrich his family made him profoundly happy. He enjoyed Mark's visits even when he was not able to speak a word and had to write his responses on a pad. He lived just long enough that spring and early summer to finish the memoirs.

The whole country mourned the death of the great general. In New York, from the window of his publishing firm, Sam watched the tremendous parade of soldiers and citizens in Grant's honor. The final burial place of the national hero is the great tomb on Riverside Drive in New York.

Printing Grant's two-volume work and selling it by subscription meant an enormous investment by the Charles L. Webster firm. Yet Mark's estimate of returns was remarkably accurate. More than 300,000 copies of the memoirs were sold, and a large initial check was sent to Mrs. Grant.

Another biography was undertaken in the summer of 1885 by young Susy Clemens. She had begun a life of her father. It started with the statement "We are a very happy family!" and continued with a flattering description of the subject's appearance. To her he was "an extraordinarily handsome man."

Then came the telling characterization: "He is a very good man, and a very funny one; he has got a temper but we all of us have in this family. He is the loveliest man I ever saw, or ever hope to see, and oh, so absent-minded!" The model for the portrait found out that Susy was working on it and often made remarks he hoped would be quoted. But the precocious thirteen-year-old was always aware of such attempts and said so in her manuscript.

This was Mark's period of radiant prosperity. His own royalties, the publishing firm's profits, and the large fees earned by his lecture tours combined to give him such assurance that he could say to a friend, "Whatever I touch turns to gold."

Late that year, however, he touched something which was to prove heavier than lead, more worthless than the glittering mica he had once seen at a mine and believed was solid silver. This was a machine for setting type. Five years before he had been taken to see this marvel. Instantly the former printer's boy, who had set type by hand for laborious hours, knew that the machine would revolutionize printing, if perfected. James W. Paige, the inventor, was sure of success. Sam was so convinced that on the spot he had invested $3000 in the patent. Whenever he wasn't too busy to think about the matter, he dreamed that his investment would reap millions.

Five years later Paige came to the Hartford mansion for

an interview with Mr. Clemens. The inventor looked dapper, talked well, and explained just what was needed to finish work on the automatic typesetter. His enthusiastic confidence was completely effective. Both men sat there in the handsome drawing room, sharing the certainty of enormous wealth. All Sam had to do was to feed the machine $30,000 then and there. And that was what he did.

CHAPTER · · · · · · ELEVEN

Some time in 1886 Susy wrote in her biography: "Mama and I have both been very much troubled of late, because Papa, since he has been publishing General Grant's books, has seemed to forget his own books and works entirely."

Friends shared this concern. Mark Twain, author, seemed eclipsed by Sam Clemens, businessman. The Webster publishing firm, enriched by the skyrocketing sales of Grant's two-volume work, had undertaken a tremendous new project. Pope Leo XIII had granted the Webster Company the American rights to publish his biography, written with his blessing by Bernard O'Reilly. People in Europe had been amazed to learn that $600,000 had been earned by the Grant memoirs, and both the papal authorities and the publishers believed the sale of Pope Leo's biography would prove even more profitable. Charles Webster, who traveled to Rome to sign the contract, was given a princely welcome at the Vatican.

While the 600-page manuscript was being set up, General Sheridan's memoirs were also under way. Almost every day Mark wrote to the New York office to settle some detail or help his partner make a decision. Webster's health was failing and he needed constant backing up.

As for the linotype machine, it was forever in need of a few simple but expensive adjustments. Time after time Sam went to see the marvel operate and was always thrilled with its phenomenal abilities. Then he would learn that some essential part had broken or something new was needed, and the complicated model would have to be taken apart and readjusted.

Mark's creative powers might have surmounted these interruptions if he had not been so possessed by dreams of wealth. He was trying to work on a long-considered tale set in the time of King Arthur, but his interest in it was fitful. What stirred him was the belief that his business ventures were drawing him into the stream of national progress. As a publisher he had set a new record for book sales. As a supporter of the typesetter, he expected to achieve the same combination of prestige and wealth.

"The Paige Compositor," he declared in a letter to Orion, "marches alone and far in the land of human invention."

Mark once described his era as "the drive and push and rush and struggle of the living, tearing, booming Nineteenth, the mightiest of all the centuries." Of course he raved against the unscrupulous way in which great fortunes were usually made. The author of *The Gilded Age* was alarmed to see money-making set up as the national goal. His own dream was to become a millionaire by supplying products valuable to the whole country. It was a dazzling, absorbing ambition.

By the end of 1888 the Webster Publishing Company was in trouble. The biography of the Pope had brought a disappointingly small profit. Charles Webster's health had failed, and the hard-working young man who had taken his place lacked the experience to recognize or initiate profitable publishing ventures. Sam, who had no notion of taking over the management, began to wish he could get rid of this unfruitful burden.

For the typesetting machine, however, he considered no sacrifice too great. Sam was giving James Paige $3000 a month to get it ready for production. Olivia, deeply worried about this financial drain, tried to reduce the family's expenditures. Even the children were aware of the necessity. One day their nurse said she must have a new box of blacking for their shoes. "Why, Marie!" cried little Jean. "You mustn't ask for things now. The machine isn't done."

Sam's confidence in ultimate success was unshakable. On the other hand, he was unhappy about his continued inability to write. This made him hungry for evidences of popularity and prestige. They were many. Whenever he could be induced to read from his books for a charity or introduce the speaker of the evening to an audience, he received a great ovation. Yale University presented him with a Master of Arts degree. A group of notables, headed by the great Edwin Booth, invited him to be a charter member of New York's celebrated Players Club. At the White House he was a welcome guest of President Cleveland and his charming wife. Of course, letters of praise and affection poured in daily and on every possible occasion the Hartford and Boston literary groups commanded his presence.

It was the peace of his studio at Quarry Farm, however, which permitted Mark to finish his book, *A Connecticut Yankee at King Arthur's Court*. The Webster firm badly needed a best seller, and this book, the first Mark had written in five years, was launched with a tremendous splash. Most readers of today find the tale a moving revelation of Mark's deep humanity and enjoy the sweep of his imagination. It has to be admitted, nonetheless, that both its episodes and its humor are apt to turn into preposterous burlesque. American reviewers mourned the author's want of taste. English critics accused him of trying to destroy the ancient tradition of knighthood and declared his work unfit for the "cultivated classes." Although the distinguished poet and classicist, Andrew Lang, defended Mark as a "benefactor beyond most modern writers," that healing drop could not cure so deep a wound.

This bitter disappointment deepened the shadows clos-

ing around the Clemens family. Having used up all his
savings to support the typesetter's wayward struggle toward
perfection, Sam grew desperate. He tried to find a few
investors who would, after investigation of the machine,
pour out money to further its completion. But none of the
wealthy men who appraised it shared Sam's conviction
that it was a good risk. Neither was the Webster Company.
Yet Olivia was so horror-stricken at the thought of its failure that she insisted on paying $60,000 to meet its most
pressing bills. "We can't allow bankruptcy, Sam," she
protested. "It would be a disgrace!"

Sorrows took further toll of the family's fortitude. The
first loss was Olivia's brother-in-law, Theodore Crane, to
whom the family was devoted. The next year, within a
month of each other, Olivia's gentle mother and Sam's
mother, the unique Jane Clemens, also slipped from life.
Susy was now a student at Bryn Mawr College and at
home her vivid presence was sorely missed. Indeed, since
carefree hospitality could not be afforded now, joy no
longer blazed upon the hearth in the Hartford house. After
long discussion, Sam and Olivia decided to close the house
and take the children to live in Europe, where expenses
could be cut in half.

Somehow, although rheumatism was added to his other
misfortunes, Mark succeeded in writing a short novel,
The American Claimant. It was bought as a serial by the
McClure Syndicate for $12,000. He was also offered $1000
each for six European letters. "At least we can spread
butter on our bread for a while," said Sam.

Early in June, 1891, the five Clemenses and Mrs. Theodore Crane sailed for Europe. After taking treatments at Aix, hearing the Wagner festival at Bayreuth, and resting at Marienbad's health resort, they settled in Berlin for the winter. Their arrival at the German capital was hailed with warmth by old friends and noted individuals who knew Mark's books. Scientists, historians, journalists, poets, diplomats, and members of the court set invited the Clemenses to brilliant receptions and small, gay parties.

Such adulation was wonderfully comforting. But it was at the quiet town of Nauheim that Mark could return to writing. He began *Tom Sawyer Abroad*, with much of his old enthusiasm, and wrote several short stories in addition to his articles. What cheered them all was a doctor's pronouncement that a heart condition of Olivia's was not serious and that she could count on regaining her health.

One of their longer stays in Europe was at the Villa Viviani, overlooking the city of Florence. The villa was just the place to free Mark's imagination from material problems. He began a piece of work he had dreamed of doing since he was thirteen years old. Flung at his feet by the wind, a page from a book had introduced the boy to Joan of Arc, and through the years, whenever possible, he had studied the records of fifteenth-century France and its glorious heroine. Now he began to write Joan's biography. Those weeks in Florence became a precious memory to Sam. When their radiant peace was broken, it was never mended again.

Early in 1893 a financial panic swept across the United States. Banks failed. Business houses and factories had to close. Railroad companies went bankrupt. The mighty lords of finance, however, profited from the disaster by buying oil wells and railroads at bargain rates. Most Americans were agonized by the fear of losing their homes, farms, and savings. Sam had to hurry back to New York to judge his situation. He didn't stay long, because there was nothing he could do. To his family he made the most of the fact that a Chicago firm was planning to produce fifty linotype machines like the Paige model. But during the next months nothing was heard of the typesetter.

"Sam," said Olivia one summer day, in a frightened voice, "we are spending the last of our capital, aren't we?" They were. Mark's royalties were pledged to creditors, and since the depression had hit the Langdon Company very hard, Olivia's income was dangerously shrunken. With deceptive calmness they told the girls that they couldn't afford to stay at the Villa Viviani any longer. They took rooms in Munich and in late August Sam made his second trip to New York.

There he stayed in the cheapest room of the Players Club. He made a brave pretense of enjoying the friends he met there. But when alone, facing the figures which showed income and outgo, capital and debt, he felt surrounded by the Furies of worry, fear, and regret. Although the publishing firm was earning nothing, the manager would not agree to Mark's plea to sell the entire business. He was still trying to mend its fortunes. Paige was another determined optimist. He shed crocodile tears because the Chicago company had delayed production of the typesetter, but was as buoyant as a balloon about its future.

Baffled, frightened, exhausted, Sam felt as if he were lost in the cave at Hannibal, wandering forlorn with no sign of a way out. Then, unheralded, there came toward him a man holding a bright lamp with an offer to lead him to outer air. The rescuer was Mr. H. H. Rogers, a brilliant financier connected with the Standard Oil Company. When this eminent man, always a great admirer of Mark Twain's books, learned through a common friend that Mark was in trouble, he at once offered his advice. Manfully Sam tried to refuse such a favor from a busy man. "Not my dreadful tangles!" he protested. But the financier said genially, "Why not leave them all to me?"

From then on he acted as Sam's business representative. First he attempted to estimate the real value of the linotype invention. He was impressed with its uncanny ability, but he knew it would have to pass severe practical tests before financial backing could be expected. The typesetter was installed in the *Times-Herald* building in Chicago for this final experiment. Rogers then took up the affairs of the Webster Publishing Company. His first act was to remove the firm's largest white elephant by arranging the sale of the *Library of American Literature* for $50,000. It provided a reprieve from immediate bankruptcy.

To hand over his lonely burden of responsibility to this

generous wizard meant intoxicating relief to Sam. In his exuberant way he was ready to plunge into any form of gaiety—all-night parties, playing billiards with Mr. Rogers, or a sumptuous luncheon at the Lotus Club. Moreover, while he was in New York he wrote several short stories and articles. His novel, *Pudd'nhead Wilson*, was being published serially in *Century Magazine* and *Tom Sawyer Abroad* was appearing in *St. Nicholas*. During a brief reunion with his family, he brought them fresh hope.

He had returned to his biography of Joan of Arc and was deep in the great trial at Rouen when a fresh crisis required his presence in New York. The Webster Publishing Company had completely collapsed. Its credit was exhausted and Mr. Rogers declared that bankruptcy was inescapable. With quiet authority he dictated the settlements. Mrs. Clemens was named the chief creditor and Mark Twain's royalties were safeguarded from claims. The assets of the company were divided among the creditors and each of them was promised a payment of fifty cents on the dollar, to be made as soon as possible.

For a very short time Sam hoped against hope that the linotype invention might prove its merit. The opposite took place. It was finally proved to be entirely too complicated and delicate to be in the least reliable. It had to be abandoned as a total loss. To be shorn of this illusion on which he had spent thousands upon thousands of dollars, was a major operation for Sam. Recovery was all the more difficult because the future he now had to face was the very one he had tried to provide against.

Instead of being a millionaire, he was a poor man encumbered with enormous debts. To pay them off meant hard, unceasing toil when he had dreamed of ease. His family, for whom he had expected to provide luxurious comfort, must live as cheaply as possible. The pride in her husband which Olivia had gradually achieved had been destroyed by the humiliating public failure of his firm.

Pacing his small New York bedroom, Sam looked back to other times when his pockets had been empty. Then, however, he had been young and strong and alone with his fate. And now? Could he ever take the family back to the beloved Hartford house? He had wickedly risked their security, and lost. Only a few years ago there had been plenty of money to give each one of them a pleasant life. His greed and his stubborn ambition had brought ruin upon them. How could he have been so blind to reality?

This agonizing self-examination left scars beneath an outer calm. When he rejoined the family—this time in Paris—he looked older and sadder, but the artist in him eagerly set to work on the last chapters of *Personal Recollections of Joan of Arc*. Olivia and the girls found the story absorbing and their enthusiasm inspired his intention to devote himself only to sound projects in literature.

What Susy had once said about her father in the unfinished biography expressed what she felt in that winter of 1895. As a little girl she had written: "[Papa] is known to the public as a humorist, but he has much more in him that is earnest than that is humorous. . . . He is as much a philosopher as anything, I think. . . . In a great many

such directions he has greater ability than in the gifts which
made him famous."

It was this earnestness which led Sam to a dual decision
before facing Mr. Rogers in New York again. Sam had
concluded that his only honorable course was to make a
full payment, dollar for dollar, to each of his creditors.
To achieve this, he intented to accept an urgent call from
Major Pond in Boston to go on a lecture tour under his
management. Mark decided, however, that the tour should
extend all the way around the world. "It's the quickest
way for me to make money," he declared at the family
council, "and the trip will provide material for another
travel book, also."

Olivia warmly approved the integrity of her husband's
decision and planned to take the world trip with him.
Although her heart ached with longing to return to the
Hartford house, she was glad at least to spend two months
at Quarry Farm in the spring and early summer. Of course
her daughters were with her and so was Sam, except for
conferences in New York. He had renewed his relation-
ship with Bliss of the American Publishing Company and
had promised him his next book. But the biography of Joan
was to be serialized in *Harper's Magazine*. Mr. Rogers
took a hand in making agreements between the two publishers. Sam told him that he would send him, from every
stop on the long journey, as much money as could be
spared. "I believe I can pay off my creditors in two years'
time," he said.

Clara was to go on the tour with her parents. Neither Susy nor Jean felt strong enough for such an effort and they were to stay with Mrs. Crane in Elmira. Major Pond planned to accompany Mr. and Mrs. Clemens and Clara as far as the Pacific coast. On July 14 the rest of the family gathered at the Elmira station to see the party off. As Sam watched Susy waving her handkerchief in loving farewell, he clutched his wife's hand and said, "Livy, I'm homesick right now!"

How he fared on the fourteen-month journey, and what he learned and enjoyed, Mark Twain told in *Following the*

Equator, a pleasant, picturesque, and sympathetic account of the countries he saw and the people he met. He did not mention the success of his lectures. In South Africa and India, as well as in Australia and New Zealand, he spoke to mammoth crowds who greeted him with intense and friendly interest. Everywhere the party was elaborately entertained and showered with gifts. During this tour Sam adopted the custom of wearing white suits, and gradually he made it his practice to wear only white, both winter and summer.

Naturally the lectures, train trips, and constant dealings with strangers combined to weary the indefatigable Mark, as well as his two companions. They all loved the long ocean trip back to England. The sight of Southampton and the comfortable train to London brought them a great sense of relief in having reached a homelike and familiar place at last.

August, 1896, was the time, and London the place, of Sam's farewell to the joy of living. All during the voyage his eyes had ached for a first glimpse of Susy. She and Jean and a faithful maid were to meet them in England. But at London the Clemenses found only a letter reporting that Susy was ill. They cabled for more news, but none came. They had to make a quick decision as to what to do. It seemed best that Mrs. Clemens and Clara should board a ship leaving for America the next day. Sam was commissioned to find a house, not too far from London, suitable for the sick girl's convalescence. So it was with no one to share his grief that Sam received the cable announcing Susy's death, while her mother and sister were still at sea.

Alone for several weeks before Olivia brought back Clara, Jean, and the maid, Sam wrestled with a wild rebellion of grief. Like Job, he cried out, "For the arrows of the Almighty are within me . . . the terrors of God do set themselves in array against me." It was, of course, a comfort to have the family with him, in the house they had taken in Chelsea. But they saw few people and scarcely went out at all.

Mark had to begin work on his travel book, and to his surprise he found he liked doing it. To see in memory the mountains of India and the South African veldt diverted his thoughts to beauty, and the very impersonality of his subject had a soothing effect upon him. But the daily notes he kept in his small black book revealed the frantic grief and despair which assailed him whenever he was not at work.

Gradually the Clemenses began to see their friends. When Mark had finished his travel book and sent it off to the American Publishing Company, the family went to Switzerland for the summer. Vienna was their choice for the winter, and the charm of its cultured society lured them into rewarding evenings of conversation and music. Clara was especially happy there. In January, 1898, came the great news from Mr. H. H. Rogers that all Sam's debts were paid.

"Livy darling!" he cried triumphantly. "Think of having no financial weight upon us!"

Livy laughingly quoted Pudd'nhead Wilson's warning. "Remember this, Sam? 'There are two times in a man's life when he should not speculate: when he can't afford it and when he can.' "

She was delighted when, at informal gatherings, Sam's spontaneous wit and humorous turns of phrase bubbled up. But she knew that when he walked alone in the public parks or sat at his desk trying to write, he would often be impelled to curse the strange impulses which had led him into folly. Denying that earthly existence was worth while, he would fill his notebooks with attacks on the human race and denials that a loving God would permit the bitter experiences which innocent individuals had to suffer.

Lovely little Jean had become subject to strange attacks and these were finally diagnosed as epilepsy. Her parents took her to Sweden, where special medical aid did help, but never cured her. During this melancholy period Sam learned of Orion's death. Often Mark had said, "Death is the only dignity left to man," and he did not grieve. Yet he keenly missed the loving brother who even from far away had shared or followed all the many different phases of his life.

October 6, 1900, found the Clemens family on the steamship *Minnehaha* bound for New York. For many years they had been moving from one place to another in

Europe and they looked forward to settling in their own land. Olivia longed to reopen the old house in Hartford, and now they could afford to do so. Mark's royalties had built up a small fortune, which Mr. Rogers doubled by wise investments. Yet without Susy the spirit of the place would be lacking. Besides, Livy had become too much of an invalid to manage house and garden as she used to love to do.

The arrival of Mark Twain in New York was a stirring event. Newspapers had published the story of how, by courageous effort and matchless talent, he had paid every debt. The city gave him a hero's welcome. When the family was established in a house on West Tenth Street, just off Fifth Avenue, Mark was besieged by friends, editors, and reporters. His interest in people and his gift for enjoying the moment brightened those autumn days. Always something of an actor, Mark loved the sensation he made by appearing in a white suit, topped on icy days by a fur coat.

New York, however, lacked the quiet which Olivia needed. After a pleasant summer in the Adirondacks, the Clemenses settled in a house in Riverdale-on-Hudson and that was their residence for three years. It was an ideal place for an invalid, yet Livy grew steadily worse.

These years reveal Sam Clemens as a man doing his best to play his assigned part with courage and good will. Old friends from near and far were welcomed with affection. Several times he voyaged on the yacht of his friend and counselor, Mr. Rogers. He made speeches at banquets and luncheons. He contributed a number of stories and articles to magazines and newspapers. Yale University gave him a second degree and so did the University of Missouri. Sam had dreaded the long trip to Missouri, but when he was met at St. Louis by Horace Bixby, the man who had taught him the ways of the Mississippi, he felt deeply rewarded. At Hannibal John Briggs, one of the pirate gang, guided him to the well-remembered spots where danger, mischief, and fun had lain in wait.

The fact that the Clemenses had a comfortable fortune once more helped to lessen Sam's self-reproach. But nothing could lift the sorrowful burden of Olivia's illness. In the fall of 1903 her doctors advised Sam to take her to Italy, where the climate had agreed with her. So with Jean, Clara, and a nurse he managed to get her there and establish them all in a fine old Florentine villa. The household was completely regulated by Livy's uncertain health. In June of the next year her tired heart ceased its efforts.

Although they had all been prepared for this possibility, the shock was crushing. Sam felt that he had no longer any reason for living. Naturally, he was deeply touched by the multitude of cables and letters sent him from around the globe. And of course he tried to hide his desolation and give comfort to his daughters.

The depth of his loneliness was poignantly expressed in a letter to Howells. "We excuse ourselves from all the friends that call—though of course, only intimates come. Intimates—but they are not the old, old friends, the friends

of the old, old times when we laughed. Shall we ever laugh again? If I could only see a dog that I knew in the old times and could put my arms around his neck and tell him all, everything, and ease my heart!"

From the time of Olivia's death the outer facts of Mark Twain's life seem less important than the ceaseless strife within his consciousness. His winter home was on lower Fifth Avenue. On a hill near Redding, Connecticut, he had built a lovely country residence, including, of course, a billiard room. It was in this spacious abode that his daughter Clara was married one October day in 1909 to the internationally famous musician, Ossip Gabrilo-witsch. This happy occasion, which deeply delighted Sam, was followed just before Christmas that same year by the sudden death of Jean.

The only really rewarding event in those years was Mark Twain's receipt of an LL.D. degree from Oxford University, the loftiest literary honor which England can bestow. The date of the ceremony was June 26, 1907. Before and after it Mark was entertained, and praised in speeches and journals. His photograph in doctor's robe and hat appeared in newspapers throughout Europe and America.

Just the year before this superb tribute Mark had decided to undertake the writing of an autobiography. His chief aid in the enterprise was a new young friend, Albert Bigelow Paine. Later Paine, on whom Mark finally depended for companionship and service, became both the literary executor of Mark Twain's writings and his chief biographer. It was he who suggested that the author might try dictating his biography. Together Paine and an equally devoted secretary spent morning after morning on the entertaining job.

From the first Mark made it clear that he was not going to deal out a conventional, year by year account of himself. He simply talked about whatever came into his head. On Monday he might be telling of the time he tossed a ripe melon down on his brother's head from an upper window. Then on Tuesday he might spend an hour raging against some current political measure. Propped up on the pillows of a bed so enormous that he was always losing his glasses or some precious clippings in its covers, tossing back his magnificent white hair, he was probably the most picturesque figure ever faced by a young lady with a stenographic notebook.

With his complete works being published by the American Publishing Company, and short pieces appearing in magazines and journals, Mark Twain was still regarded by the public as an active writer. But he himself characterized his last years as "washing about in a forlorn sea of banquets and speechmaking in high and holy causes."

Actually his pen had never been busier. Manuscripts piled up in his desk drawers. They were stories made of dreams and fantasy. All of them were dedicated to the same theme—the helplessness of man. He pictured human beings as involved in some sort of struggle but, as in a typical nightmare, inevitably doomed to failure and consequent suffering. Since such was man's dark destiny, could he possibly be blamed for mistakes, defeat, and sin?

Samuel Clemens, worn out with the weight of guilt he had carried since he was a little boy, longed to say no to this question. He longed to put the blame for misdeeds outside the realm of human will. Men, he believed, were drawn into evil by a force stronger than they are. It was not God, but the devil who ruled, by deceiving mankind and putting conscience to sleep. He, not man, must be accused. Mark kept trying to express dramatically this explanation of wrongdoing. Over and over again he put aside his efforts as a failure.

Even those closest to Mark Twain never guessed that such a struggle was going on. They thought his angers at the Deity and at the race of men were no more than sardonic twists of humor. His warmhearted affection for friends, his unfailing kindness and his ability to give and to take pleasure, completely hid his inner torment. He felt that it could only be relieved by a powerful presentation of the truth as he saw it.

Finally inspiration came to him. He wrote a fairy tale which symbolized his repudiation of God and man. This strange jewel of a book lay among the scraps and tag ends of unfinished manuscripts. At last he had succeeded—too well, his publishers thought. For years they did not dare present to the public this story, which is all the more terrible because of its beauty. Yet when *The Mysterious Stranger* appeared in print, it was at once acclaimed as a work of art. The author never knew this. It was published after his death.

On April 21, 1910, at Stormfield, his peaceful country place, Samuel Clemens breathed his last. Although he was buried beside his wife in the Elmira cemetery, a public funeral was held first in a New York church. There, on his last narrow bed, lay the slim figure clad in his favorite white flannels, to receive the farewells of the hundreds who filed slowly by. If he could have read their thoughts, he would have found them full of gratitude for the joy he had given to everyone who knew him, to all who knew his books. And they must also have been proud of the man who typified the spirit of America in his humor and in his life, with its youthful adventures, its abrupt rise to fame and fortune, its spell of extravagance, and its victory over failure.

Such was the popular feeling about Samuel Langhorne Clemens. Several literary commentators, however, have presented him as a tragic figure. They declare that the writer whose work fills volume after volume achieved only three creations of high artistic merit: *The Adventures of Tom Sawyer, The Adventures of Huckleberry Finn,* and *The Mysterious Stranger.* The author is accused of having wasted his gifts for unjustifiable reasons and having failed to keep faith with his genius.

One critic states that Mark Twain strikingly represents the perils besetting American artists who become famous in any field. Few of them can stand success. In this country publicity and financial rewards all too often lure gifted individuals from that lonely realm of the spirit where inspiration can be received. Adulation of personality such as that received by Mark is intoxicating to the human ego. As a result the connection with the true source of artistic creation is broken.

Mark himself might very likely have agreed with this appraisal. More painful than the devastating sorrows which he endured was the inner knowledge that he had placed worldly success above his responsibility as an artist. Yet it should be remembered that he was a man who experienced love on every level and let it shine through his writing. His hates were magnificently hurled against human selfishness and stupidity in all their forms and wherever he found them, not sparing himself. Completely devoid of that numbness concerning events and people which deadens the spirit, he cared deeply how his country was governed and how his fellow men fared. Even his terrifying portrait of the glamorous devil who denied the validity of earthly life is a stern challenge to the sleeping consciousness of mankind. In spite of his disbelief in the existence of spiritual beings, Mark Twain as man and author, was on their side.

JEANETTE EATON was born in Columbus, Ohio, and was brought up in a household where books and music, friends and a garden, were enjoyed and valued. She was graduated from Vassar College and received her master's degree from Ohio State University. After trying different jobs in various parts of the United States, she wrote stories and articles for magazines and newspapers before settling down to write books for young people, a field to which she now devotes herself almost entirely. "Biography for young people is my vocation," she says. "It is a choice one, which permits constant association with the great people of this earth." In her many fine biographies, Miss Eaton has made it possible for her readers to enjoy the same wonderfully good company. She writes about people who are not only famous but extremely interesting, and she tells their stories with contagious enthusiasm.